Follow

POS/Dry Cleaning Software for Windows

Users Guide

Manual Version 1.00
Software Version 15.11.xx or Higher

www.FollowPOS.com
Follow Dry cleaning Software – *Users Guide*
Dry Cleaning Software Provider Since 1987

Copyright 1984 - Revised 2009, 2013 **– Follow Systems**
FollowSystems.com
Revised 11/17/2014

Table of contents

Introduction

Welcome

Getting Started – Quick Overview

Congratulations on your purchasing Follow, the Dry Cleaning Software package that's designed to be a local or cloud based Point of Sale System, a versatile Windows Software package for Dry Cleaners and Stores on the market today.

Follow – A Visual Difference

Follow comes with a complete installation system that will analyze your system and configure Follow for the type of computer you have.

The Installation program for Follow is located at: www.FollowPOS.com found under the downloads link.

Buttons and Navigation

Follow works with a simple menu that is always returned to after each transaction.

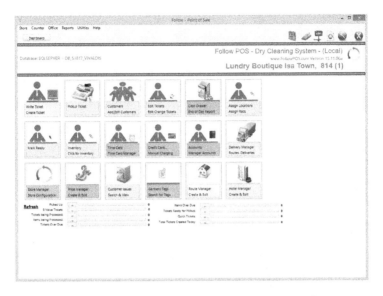

To use Follow Simply click one of the buttons from the main menu.

1. Write a Ticket – will allow you to write for a new ticket for a customer as well as add a new customer
2. Pickup Tickets - will allow you to pick up tickets for a customer
3. Edit Ticket - allows you to change or reprint any ticket already created in the system
4. Customers – allows you to add customers or change customer information
5. Customer History – select this option to view customer tickets
6. Assign Location – select this option to assign the rack number to a ticket
7. Mark Tickets Ready – select this option if you do not assign rack numbers to a ticket and you simply wish to mark the ticket as ready for pickup
8. Accounts – Allows you to print statement, make payments or modify accounts receivable

9. Inventory – select this option to scan inventory to find missing tickets
10. Delivery Management – select this option to print and process delivery tickets
11. Time Card – will link to an external time card system
12. End of day Report – select this option to print the current days report
13. Cash Drawer – select this option to z out the drawer at the end of the day
14. Price lookup – allows you to look up prices in the system
15. Cash Drawer – allows you to enter starting cash, adjustments and Z out the Drawer at the end of the day.
16. X-Charge – Access the X-Charge system directly to refund or process credit cards directly trhough the x-charge system (Requires signup and setup by the x-charge support).
17. Store Manager – Modify Store Name, Address, Phone number and Program configuration information.
18. Garment Tags – allows you search garment tag numbers to find tickets.
19. Hotel Manager – Add and change Hotel information for hotels you delivery to.
20. Route Manager – allows you to add, change and manage your delivery routes.
21. Customer Issues – allows you to record and search customer issues.

A Simple walk through....

The Follow System has been designed with more flexibility than any system on the market today. To understand how complex the system is and versatile you will need to read the later sections in this manual, but to start with let's begin with the basic System. Let's assume that you have installed Follow on your computer and you have clicked on the icon or selected the menu option from Start – Program Files – Follow. You have the basic system up on your window.

Now what do you do.... Begin by following the steps below to follow what a typical counter person would need to do on a daily basis.

Follow Systems

Follow is one of the first and oldest Dry Cleaning Software Companies offering POS - Delivery - Email Notification - Web Interface - Remote Access - Credit Card Processing -Customized Ticket by Customer- Auto Offsite Backup - Multi store uploading - Hotel Valet - Loyalty System with auto Coupons - Cash Drawer -

We have been selling Dry Cleaning Software for over 25 years. One of the oldest Dry Cleaning Software companies on the market. While the other companies come and go we are still there. Follow software runs on any Windows computer that you purchase or already have. We can also send you a fully loaded system already configured and ready to run or you can purchase just the software to run on a computer you purchase locally.

Our Classic Packages are great systems that will work the way you work for years to come and includes the software, a Windows 7,8 64 bit computer, Touch Screen monitor, Thermal printer, Tag Printer, barcode reader, automatic cash drawer and 30 days voice support and a year of free upgrades and email support. Affordable and Easy to use Dry Cleaning Software!

We are more than a POS Company we are you Dry Cleaning Consultants ... With a system to support you and organize your business.

90% of your sales come from 10% of your customers. Our system shows you how to increase sales within that model and build your business in a tight economy.

Contact Us

Follow Systems Sales Office

www.FollowPOS.com
Hesperia, California
USA
760-524-2473
International Sales: 760-524-2473
sales@Followsystems.com
Sales Manager

Support

Follow Support Office
Email Now support@Followsystems.com
760-282-4421
support@Followsystems.com
Support Manager

Credit Card Processing

Credit Card Processing through Follow X-CHARGE
Philip Head - 1202 High Tech Circle Henderson,
Nevada 89015
www.Acceleratedpay.com
(800) 637-8268 x111
Fax:(702) 446-8145
philip.head@acceleratedpay.com

Hardware Purchases and Support

Hardware Quotes MS Cash drawer
Tanya - 2085 East Foothill Blvd. Pasadena, CA 91107
www.mscashdrawer.com
Email Now Attn: Tanya Doubko
tdoubko@mscashdrawer.com
(800) 544-1749
Fax: (626) 792-4033
tdoubko@mscashdrawer.com

Features

- Full install and uninstall support for windows 95, 98, NT, XP, 2000 and 2003, Windows 7 and 8 both 32 and 64 bit systems.
- Customizable System to work the way you do
- CD-ROM installation
- Built In Credit Card Processing
- Password protection and user access control
- Station Access control allowing you to customize each computer station in your store to have only the access you want
- Integrated online help
- Designed to work with the mouse or keyboard for quick Ticket entry
- Customizable reports and Report Writer for adding and customizing Reports
- Works with any Windows Compatible printer
- Works with all Barcode readers
- Integrated Automatic Credit Card processing
- Point and Click functionality
- Intuitive Interface
- Fully Functional Dry cleaning Software inclusive of all the modules you will ever need
    - Simple easy to use
    - Fast Ticket Generation
    - Network Ready
    - Multi locational
    - Quick easy to use Item pricing windows
    - Forced upcharges with popup Windows forcing your counter people to think about up charging
    - Option Upcharges with pull down windows
    - Individual Item lists for hundreds of Item Classes allowing you to arrange special pricing for Customer Groups, VIPs, Hotels, Wholesales, Dry Stores, Offices, Special organizations, etc.
    - Tickets printed with optional bar code for fast inventory and pickup

- Pickup with barcode
- Drop off with barcode customer VIP cards for accuracy and speed
- Versatile Item and upcharge menus allowing pricing changing on the spot
- Describe and price during invoicing.
- Quick change of class
- Quick reprinting of tickets
- Prepayment capabilities
- Special (1 day service/VIP Customers)
- Discounts for customers or groups
- Unlimited number of items in the system
- Unlimited number of orders and items per invoice
- Garment Tag system built in
- Continuous Form feed Tickets
- Laser Tickets
- Laser Printed Reports
- Preview on screen, Tickets and Reports
- Pickup multiple tickets for customer
- Indicates type of package – box, hanger
- Box labels printed
- Delivery system built in (hundreds of routes and hundreds of stops)
- Deliver Manifest with automatic billing to Accounts Receivable or Credit Card
- Automatic Accounts Receivable module built in with Laser printed statements
- Charge on Credit card and automatically batch to the bank
- Check writing capability and recording to the daily cash drawer and deposit report
- Color monitoring
- Fabric up charges
- Monitors date Out and time for future reference
- Tracks customer sales for Sales reports and customer labels for cards, discounts or personal letters
- Fully integrated Hotel management delivery system with Hotel Manifest and General ledger statements, manages comps, schedules, billing, etc...

- Fully integrated wholesale system with separate pricing and statements
- Fully integrated Cash drawer with cash reconciliation reports
- Credit limit monitoring
- Production reports
- Security controlled menus
- Automatic backup system
- Separate menu for Archive Tickets for reference
- Hundreds of reports
- Fully integrated Home delivery system
- Outside processing
- Quick drop off tickets
- Inventory Control system
- Uniform System
- Multi-Store Replication
- Enterprise management system
- General Ledger Accounts Assignments
- Loyalty System
- Pricing levels

Customer Service and Marketing

- Auto Email Customers
- Email Marketing Coupons, newsletters, Customer Welcome Letters
- Text messages and Email when Orders are Ready
- Reminders to Pick up old Ticket
- Link with mail Chimp and Constant Contact
- Automatic Loyalty Dollars and Coupons printed
- Keeps track of Customers Loyalty Dollars
- Color code customers on each screen (VIP, Loyalty, Absent Customers, New Customers, Customers who have hit certain threshold of Dollars)

Why Follow

So you've decided to install a computer system in your Store. The first step is to decide how you want your system to work for you. We need to begin with an evaluation of the goals of the system. Take a moment and think about what you want this system to do for your operation over the course of the next few years. The Follow system is packed with all the features you will ever need from ticket writing to Accounts receivable, delivery system, valet, and even the web interface for customer delivery. Follow Modules are all included in one package. You don't need to install everything at once but decide which modules are most important to begin then add additional hardware and features in the future. The software includes all the features for one price, so there is no need to upgrade or purchase more modules when you're ready to grow your system.

Here are a few ideas to begin focusing on:

- Increase profits
- Increase organization in the production side
- Get a better picture of how your company is doing
- Increase customer satisfaction
- Increase efficiency and speed
- Monitor your employees better
- Start a Delivery service
- Begin delivering to Hotels
- Start Wholesale work and billing
- Offer Accounts and Statements to Customer
- Begin using a loyalty or Gift card service
- Start a monthly email newsletter with coupons.
- Start emailing customer Tickets and Pickup reminders
- Start a website with customer access of tickets with home delivery signup.
- Start an internet marketing campaign

   Now that you've had time to think we can spend time setting your system up to accomplish these goals.
- The Follow System needs some information from you before it can be run. These are the setup procedures. On the next few pages is a setup questionnaire that you need to fill out. These questions relate to how you do business and how you thing this system would work best to increase your profits and customer satisfaction.
- The first set of questions relate to the price listing. These decisions are not set in gold and can be

changed later, even daily. That's the beauty of the system, prices and upcharges can be changed online anytime you wish and the changes are instantly active. To begin, use the form below to decide which items will receive which prices and how you want these items broken into classes and sub items.

- One of the advantages with a computer system is it will allow you to separate the cost effective items and non-cost effective ones and analyze each daily. You want to monitor the items that are costing more to run through your store and perhaps assign upcharges to recoup some costs. To do this you need to discover what differences these items have that take more time to clean and place upcharges that correspond such as silk or white (could be an extra 25 cents). An example of this would be a silk shirt with grease marks on the sleeve. The shirt would be a standard item on the item listing but the silk would upcharge a dollar or so and the grease would upcharge another dollar for spotting.

If you have not yet purchased the Follow System and wish to install a demo to play with the system before purchasing, follow the Installing the Demo instructions below. You can also find the links and instructions on the FollowPOS.com Demo Download link. http://FollowPOS.com/demo.html

Installing the Demo

Step 1: Install Client Software Metro

New POS Metro Dry Cleaning System Client.

Download the Follow 8 Metro Cloud Version (SQL Server Based) Clicking here!

http://followpos.com/install.html

1. Install the setup.msi by clicking on the link above. (Then install the upgrade by unzipping the Followupgrade.exe to the C:\Follow folder)
2. Login as a demo user email address: rick2164@msn.com password: 2164 Store #: 1

This Follow will allow you to run your store from anywhere with an internet connection, great for Tablets (Requires Windows 8 Tablets only - Windows Surface Pro)

Step 2: Upgrade Client Software for Metro

Upgrade a current install of POS Metro Point of Sale to the Latest Version by Clicking Here. Free Upgrade for registered users and Demo Users.

Download the Upgrade by Clicking here!

http://www.FollowPOS.com/upgrade.exe

(Requires that the Follow 8 Metro Client or full system Software be Installed first. Upgrades for Follow are always free.)

Upgrading Follow

Download the Upgrade by Clicking here!

http://www.FollowPOS.com/Followupgrade.exe

(Requires that the Follow 8 Metro Client or full system Software be Installed first)

Regional Settings for the Date format need to be MM/DD/YYYY

And The ODBC Settings are needed to run reports (Support will help with these)

Getting Started

System requirements

Follow is a completely Visual system designed to complement your way of doing business. All the menus have been designed to allow for quick intuitive access to the Follow options. Follow is a 32 and 64 bit Windows Application programmed in C++ and capable of running on any Vista, XP, Windows 95, 98, NT or 2000, Windows 7 and Windows 8 or 10 computer.

We recommend at least a Pentium system preferably a with min. 2 gigs of RAM. The Hard drive requirements for Follow are minimum. 5 gigs of space is plenty.

We Recommend Windows 10 64 bit with Follow.

- Windows 7 or 8 -64 or 32 Bit is recommended with a Min Requires min of 2 gigs of RAM
- 50 g Hard drive
- Monitor with min resolution 1024 by 768 (Follow Metro requires higher resolutions if you want to view more data)
- Microsoft Vista is not recommending

We strongly recommend that you run Follow on 64 bit Windows 7 or Windows 8 to avoid performance issues.

XP – Requires min of 1 gig of RAM

Any version of Windows will work.

Hardware Packages

Our Classic Dry Cleaning Packages and include the software, a Windows 7 & 8 32/64 bit computer, Touch Screen monitor, Thermal printer, Tag Printer, barcode reader, automatic cash drawer and 30 days voice support and a year of free upgrades and email support. *Affordable and Easy to use Dry Cleaning Software.*

Our Classic Dry Cleaning Packages include the Follow Professional software, Two Windows 7 & 8 32/64 bit computer Dell Business Computers, 1 Touch Screen monitor and 1 non touch Screen 19" Flat Screen monitor,1 Thermal printer,1 Tag Printer,1 barcode reader,1 automatic cash drawer and 30 days voice support and a year of free upgrades and email support. *Affordable and Easy to use Dry Cleaning Software - You need a hub or internet router at the location to connect the computer to. (Hub and network cables not included)*

Starter Dry Cleaning Packages Dell Business Windows 7 & 8 32/64 bit Computer & Flat screen Monitor , Follow Professional Software, Automatic Cash drawer, Barcode Reader and Star Thermal Ticket Printer Call Today: 760.524.2473 - Total Prices no gimmicks. Comes with the Follow Professional Software.

Starter Dry Cleaning Packages Dell Business Windows 7 & 8 32/64 bit Computer & Flat 15" Touch screen Monitor , Follow Professional Software, Automatic Cash drawer, Barcode Reader and Star TSP100 Thermal Ticket Printer Call Today: 760.524.2473 - Total Prices no gimmicks. Comes with the Follow Professional Software.

Follow Professional Dry cleaning Software only is priced at $995 (This month's special $395.00) a store. Unlimited stations in 1 location. This price includes the full featured System and 1 year of free technical email support as well as online training and installation up to 4 hours. (2 hours of conversion of current data if possible) 1 year of free upgrades. - Email Module comes free with the Follow Professional System.

Hardware

POS Metro Cloud 2 Station Package $2295

The 2 station Dell All in One Touch Screen System - consists of
Qty 2 - Dell All in One Touch Screen Computer or Separate PC and Monitor 7 & 8 32/64 Systems
Qty 1 - Thermal Ticket Printer (Star TSP100)
Qty 1 - Automatic Cash drawer
Qty 1 - Barcode Reader
Qty 1 - Tag Printer (Star SP700 or Epson U220)
2 Hours Installation and Training (Remote)(plus $9.95 a month Hosting and Support)
(Both stations share the printers and cash drawer)
1 Store License of Follow 8 POS Metro Cloud software (unlimited stations)

POS Metro Cloud 2 Station and Tablet Package $2795

The 2 station Dell All in One Touch Screen System - consists of
Qty 2 - Dell All in One Touch Screen Computer,
Qty 1 - Thermal Ticket Printer (Star TSP100)
Qty 1 - Automatic Cash drawer
Qty 1 - Barcode Reader
Qty 1 - Tag Printer (Star SP700)
2 Hours Installation and Training (Remote)
(plus $9.95 a month Hosting and Support) (Both stations share the printers and cash drawer)
1 Store License of Follow 8 POS Metro Cloud software (unlimited stations)
and the Asus Windows 8 Tablet for Accessing Follow 8 on the Road or home. 2 Hours Installation and Training (Remote)(plus $9.95 a month Hosting and Support)

Computers

The Dell All in One Touch Screen System - Dell All in One Touch Screen Computer, Thermal Ticket Printer (Star TSP100) , Automatic Cash drawer, Barcode Reader, Tag Printer (Star SP700), POS Metro Cloud 2 Hours Installation and Training (Remote)(plus $9.95 a month Hosting and Support)

Printers

$219 STAR TSP 100 Thermal USB printer with Cable. 1 Year warranty. Fast graphics thermal printer, no ink or cartridges.

$243 STAR SP 700 Impact USB printer with Cable. 1 Year warranty. Fast graphics thermal printer, no ink or cartridges.

Networking

Networking is simple with Follow Metro. Make sure each of the system has access to the internet and you will have access to the Follow Database on the cloud.

Exceptions: Make sure the firewalls allow access to SQL Server.

For speed you need to set each system up to access the internet via a cable to the network hub/router. Wireless connection do work but you will find faster access with a cable connection.

Printers

You can select the **"Select Printer"** option before printing any of the reports. All reports will print in preview mode first then the printer icon will appear in the upper left corner. After pressing the printer window the select printer option will appear to select any printer you have installed.

PRINTER SELECT BEFORE PRINTING THE TICKET

To select a printer before each ticket is printed select the Ticket Properties window by right mouse clicking on the Ticket Window. Select the Properties option. Select the Other Defaults tab then click on the "Show Ticket Printer Select before Printing".

TYPES OF PRINTERS

- Selecting your printer:
- If you choose to use the Star TSP700 Thermal printer or any other thermal printer you will need to select the ticket called "Ticket". This can be selected under the ticket properties option under the right mouse click from the main menu.   This ticket will print 1 ticket.
  - o In addition to selecting this ticket select the number of copies option and change that to 2 or 3 depending on the number of copies you want to print.
  - o The Star TSP700 prints fast if the fonts are change on the report to the default fonts of the printer.
  - o The procedure for installing this printer are as follows:
    - ▪ You will first need to load the Windows drivers for this printer. These printer drivers can be found at pos.Epson.com if you

have problems installing these drivers you will need to visit this web site or call the Epson support line

- To test the printer driver enter the notepad.exe program supplied by windows and print a few test lines.

- Once the printers print, enter Follow and select the Utilities option. Select the Report Writer option. Then press the open library button and select the folder c: driver, Follow folder then select reports. (c:\Follow\reports). Then open the Follow.rp5 file. Select the "Ticket" Report. Select File then printers and select the Epson TM 88 iii or ii printer. Then press File then Save. This will assign the Epson printer to the to the Ticket report.

- Enter the Device Settings window and select the form name as the tractor feed default form:

- If you have issues with installing forms call the support number for the printer.

Cash Drawers

Follow support automatic cash drawers that connect to the printer. Most cash drawers work this way with a cable similar to a phone cable to connect from the printer to the drawer. A file located in the c:\Follow directory named cashdrawer.bat contains the dos command to open this drawer. The batch file will send the special commands located in a text file to the printer share name.

Sample:

Type star.txt > \\localhost\Ticket

This is the typical line that would be located in the cashdrawer.bat file

The star.txt is the file containing the open drawer codes for the printer you are plugged into.

Follow includes the star.txt for the Star TSP100 printer. The second part of the command sends the file to the \\localhost (this is the name of the computer) and \Ticket (this is the share name of the printer)

Bar Code Readers

Follow ships with the idautomation39 font. It's a free font. The font is available in the c:\Follow folder called barcode.exe. Run this program and install. For configuration information look up the manufacture of this font on the web. Most readers include an automated reader that can detect the type of reader and automatically set. If your reader is not reading the barcode then

1. Check that it has an automated mode or you will need to get the configuration codes to read the font.

2. Check with the manufacture and email/fax them a copy of the font so they can send you how to configure the reader.

3. Return the reader and get an automatic reader from the FollowPOS.com website.

Borland Database Settings

Follow Needs no BDE Configuration. But does need the ODBC set to SQL Server. See ODBC

Fixing Database Corruption

The Follow Metro is based on SQL Server which has automatic backups. If you chose to use the Cloud version of Follow Metro, the administrators at Follow will back up the database and administer the servers. Including installing and updating virus software and server patches.

Sql server is a very stable database used by government, banks and businesses all over the world. There is no need to reindex or clean the database.

If you chose the local version of the database then you will need to support and manage your own database, backup, and configure.

Memory

ADJUSTING MEMORY

The total memory requirements for Follow is 2 (4 or more is even faster) gig of ram. You can run Follow with less but make sure that the Virtual Memory is set high. The procedure for setting virtual memory is laid out below.

To adjust the memory for Follow right mouse click on "My Computer" and select Properties. Then select the Advanced tab.

Select the Performance Options button. Then select the **Advanced** tab then the **Change** option. This will change the Virtual memory Value for Total paging file size, increase this size to 1024 or 2048. Then select OK.

Windows Date Format Supported

SETTING THE WINDOWS DATE FORMAT

From the **Windows** menu select **Start** then select
Control Panel. Select the **Region and Language**
settings and set the short date format to mm/dd/yyyy
this format is the only format Follow Can use.
Follow Metro does support foreign date formats.

If you are using a European date format make sure to
set the option in Region and Language under the
control panel and also set your store in Follow Store
Management to use European Format.

Getting help

Help is available on all the main windows as well as our great Youtube.com training channel with videos that will walk you through all the major functions.

Monthly newsletters are sent to each user on new features and functions.

Support is available on the Follow online chat, free email support, support@Followsystems.com, and the voice support at the support center. (760.282.4421)

Sales assistance can be found at the Sales Office 760.524.2473 or email sales@Follow2000.com (Sales Manager Rick)

There is also online chat available for free for quick questions at the website: www.FollowPOS.com

Remote Access

You will then need to go to www.AnyDesk.com or AnyDesk.com and setup a free account and "Add computer" using the computer to be installed on when it arrives.

Then email me back the email address you use and the TWO passwords you setup. Try not to get to fancy with passwords.

Please try to remember the passwords and remember they are case sensitive! So email them to us correctly!

Logmein.com does charge a yearly fee.

A free remote access program is also available at www. AnyDesk.com or AnyDesk.com Setup a free / Remote noncommercial account online. The Follow Support now uses Team Viewer and prefers this method for Support.

Tech Support

Support is available on the Follow online chat, free email support, support@Followsystems.com, and the voice support at the support center. (760.282.4421)

Purchasing the System

Purchasing the System is easy

Go to the www.FollowPOS.com site and select Packages.

Choose the package you want or call the sales office for a custom package (760.524.2473)

Press the Buy Now or Add to Cart button.

If you have a paypal.com account you can pay with that or choose the option to pay without using your paypal.com account.

After purchasing you will receive a password that will be setup with your email address to log in to the system.

If you choose a package all the items are usually ordered within 24 hours.
The Dell computer usually takes about 5 to 7 days to ship. The other items are usually shipped the next day.

You will start to receive order confirmations and tracking numbers sent to the email you used when ordering.

If the shipping address is different than the billing address you will need to email to the sales@FollowPos.com or your sales person to correct the shipping address.

Prior to shipping a confirmation of shipping address will be email giving you a chance to reply with a change of shipping address.

After the packages arrive then call the support office to arrange an appointment for the tech to install you remotely.

You will need to connect the computer to an internet temporarily for the tech to install using logmein.com (you will need to setup a free account with www.logmein.com and add the new computer)

Installing & Setting Up your System

After the packages arrive then call the support office to arrange an appointment for the tech to install you remotely.

You will need to connect the computer to an INTERNET temporarily for the tech to install using logmein.com (you will need to setup a free account with www.logmein.com and add the new computer)

Each station can be installed following the instructions for installing the client in this manual or on the download client option on the webpage.

Overview

Opening the Program

Once the application and upgrade are installed, start the application by selecting the Desktop Icon Follow 8 Metro or selecting the Follow 8 Metro program from the All Programs menu.

Logging In

Each store requires a login to enter Follow. To begin using the application enter the email address assigned to the store account. Then enter the password for the user who is logging in.

*The demo account can be accessed under
rick2164@msn.com with password: 2164

Each store has an associated email account although each user at the store must have a unique password. Follow will automatically assign the access level based on the user whose password is entered.

To add users or change user access controls select the User Manager option from the top menu.

After you purchase the Follow subscription you will be emailed a user id (which will usually be the email address that you purchased the system under and a default password. The default password can be changed under the Utilities – User Manager.

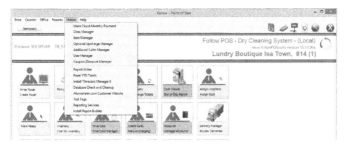

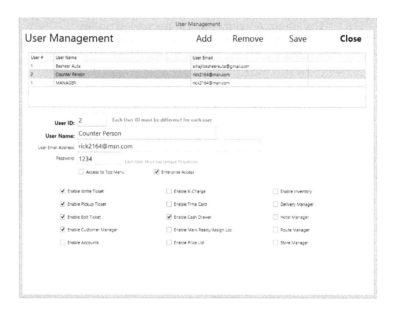

To **Manage** users select the user from the list then press the edit User button on the left.

To **Add** a new user press the Add User button on the left.

To **Remove** a user press the Delete Item button on the left.

- After you Add or Edit a user make sure to press the Save Changes button on the left.

Each user requires a unique ID #. This number will be displayed on Tickets and transaction history. The User also requires a unique Password. Each user will enter the password # before transactions and when entering the program.

To allow this user to use the top menu for accessing reports and utilities place a check in the Access to Top Menu Option.

Enterprise access is used if you have several stores connected to your account and you wish the dashboard to access all you're stores.

Along with each user you must select which options you wish the users to have. Simple check the various options that apply to this user then press Save Changes. Each user can also have an email address separate from the store email address. This would be for email the employee.

Access Levels and Security codes are for reference only and not used in Follow Metro. This is a reference for compatibility with Legacy Follow Classic.

Menu

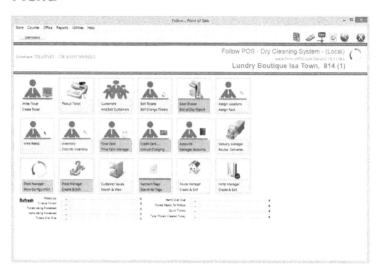

The Follow System is a purely Windows System, with a button style menu in the middle that will allow you to click on the buttons to enter a function such as Add Ticket, Pickup, Edit, etc...   You can also use the function keys on the top of the keyboard to select functions as well. The system has been designed to allow the user who is more comfortable with the mouse to use the mouse or the user who prefers to use touch screen to simple tap the large buttons.

Top Menu

The top menu is for advanced management functions. All the reports are located on the reports menu and the utilities such as Item and Price management are all located under the Utilities Menu.

All the functions for the counter person are located on the top menu and as quick access buttons located on the main menu window. Special Office functions can be found under the Office menu.

Quick additional buttons are also located on the top. (Blue buttons)

The big Red X is also the exit from the application and return to Windows.

Each of the menu and buttons can be turned on and off for each user based on the options you select for the user under the Utilities – User Manager Screen.

Main Menu Buttons

The Main menu buttons will appear and disappear depending on the user access rights. Each menu button is also connected to the top menu option for access as well.

Right Mouse content Menus

The Follow Metro does not use right mouse menus. All options for configuration are located under the Store Manager.

Menu security by User Level

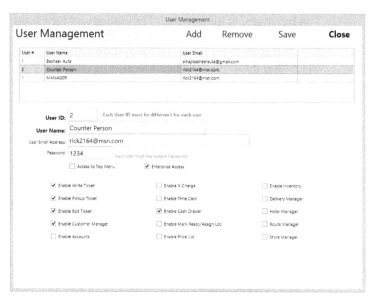

Each button and menu option is controlled by the checkboxes under the user manager under the Utilities. After you have selected the user from the Grid selected the Edit User option, change the selected options then press the Save Changes button on the left menu.

Store Overview - Dashboard

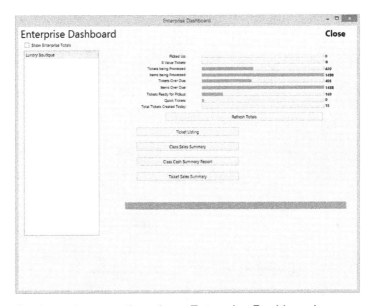

On the main menu there is an Enterprise Dashboard button on the top of the Screen called "Dashboard". This will list all the stores within the Enterprise. You have the option of selecting a store on the panel on the left then pressing the "Refresh Totals" button. To View all the totals from all the Store select the "Show Enterprise Totals" checkbox first.

Security

To use security you have several options

1. Allow the user to login once the application is first entered only.

  * To use Follow in this mode make sure the "Use Logon on Every Transaction" is turned on (no check) This will ask the user for a password only when the program first opens but not after each transaction.

  * If you have several users on the counter you will not be able to track who wrote, edited or pickup each ticket.

  * This mode is best used if you only have one counter person or you do not need to track who does which transaction.

2. Turn on the "Use Logon on Every Transaction"

  This mode is used if you want each user of the system to enter their password prior to each transaction. This will allow you to track the user and time that each event occurred.

User Control

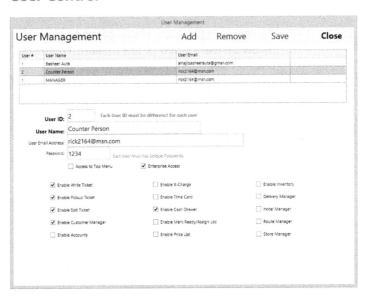

If you wish to track each user's transactions, then create a user entry for each user that will be using the system. Select the checkboxes below the user information to indicate which options you wish the user to have access to.

- Each user needs a unique ID for each store.

- Each user needs a unique password for each store. This is because Follow only requires the user to enter the password if Use logins on every transaction is turned on under the Store manager.

   To Add a new user, press the Add User button on the left, enter a new ID , Name and password, select which options the user will need then press the SAVE CHANGES button on the left.

To return to the Main menu press the left arrow on the top left of the screen. To select another user to manage press the Select User option on the left.

Access Levels

To use **Access Control** you will need to turn on the following options:

Create users under the User Management found on the Utilities menu. Set the user's level by checking the checkbox next to the function you wish the user to have.

These functional checkboxes will determine what menu option and main menu button will be available when this user logs in.

Transaction History

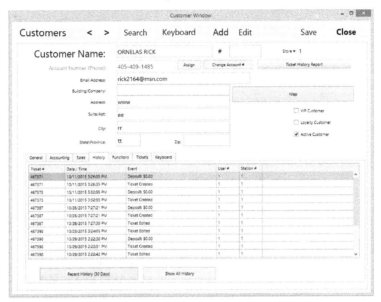

There are several types of Transaction history to view Tickets and Ticket History.

To view all the Tickets for a Customer press the Customer Management button on the main menu. Search and select a customer then select the Tickets Tab after pressing the Edit Customer button.

This window will allow you to view all the tickets for a customer.

- There is also a Ticket History Report button on the top right of the window.

To View all the History of a Ticket

Who created the ticket, Edited the ticket, assigned it's rack location , and picked up the ticket and when press the Edit Ticket button from the main menu, Search for the ticket using the criteria search area above, once you select a ticket (click once to select and highlight) then press the Ticket History button on the left.

A window will appear with all the Ticket history.

User Action History

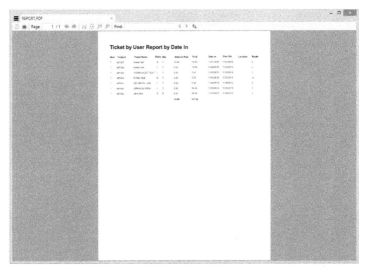

User History Report showing Ticket Sales by User

This will display each ticket and action that the user has affected for today.

Customer History

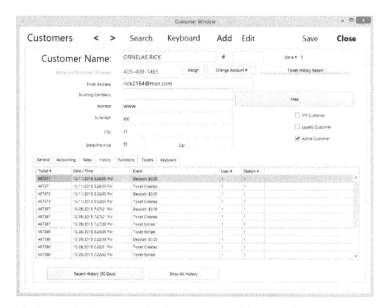

Under each Customer in the customer Manager is a tab for History. This will allow you to display all the transactions that have occurred for that customer in the last 30 days or all History. (All History will take longer to display)

Ticket History

You can view all the Ticket Transaction history by selected Edit Ticket. After you select the ticket from the Ticket search screen press the Ticket History Button on the bottom left of the menu screen.

You can also view Ticket History by customer from the Customer Manager. There is a tab for History and Transactions.

Store and Counter

Ticket Writing

ADDING A TICKET – (F2) OR PRESS ADD TICKET MENU OPTION

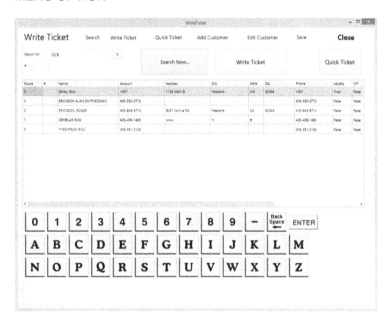

Select a Customer

Customers can be selected by left mouse clicking on the customer and highlighting the customer then pressing the button on the left button bar for the desired action or double clicking on the customer line.

On the write ticket and pickup ticket you have the option of selecting by double clicking as well.

If User Login on Each Transaction is set on then you will need to enter the users password after each transaction but the user id will be logged indicating who affected the transaction

The default search uses both alpha and numeric symbols. A customer can be found by entering either name or account number into the search bar. The system automatically recognizes if numbers or letters are entered and searches for accounts by name or account number accordingly.

There are 2 options for creating Tickets:

1. Write and itemize the complete ticket. To itemize this way press the Write Ticket button on the left after selecting the Customer or double click on the Customer name.

2. To create a Quick Ticket select the customer in the customer search window by single clicking. Then press the Quick Ticket button on the left side of the ticket.

Customer Type Indicators

The customer grid in the search area will display indicators that the customer is a VIP or Loyalty customer. In addition to this the right side of the grid will display the total amount of sales for the customer and the last time the customer was in.

Entering Items

Follow Metro uses the following process for writing Tickets.

1. Select the Quantity

2. Select the Item

3. Select the Upcharge and Color (optional)   Repeat till the ticket is completed.

4. Press the Save and Print when done

5. Select the Date of Pickup then press Print & Close.

ENTERING THE QUANTITY OF THE ITEM

To begin writing Tickets you have the option of selecting an Item first and taking the default of 1 as the quantity. If you wish to select more than 1 as the quantity for the item select the quantity on the number pad in the top left of the write ticket screen. The selected quantity will appear in yellow next to the 3 button.

To select multiple digits for the item press the "…" button.

MULTI DIGIT QUANTITY

After you select the ... button the multi digit window will appear. Enter the Quantity and press the OK button. Then select the item.

SELECTING THE ITEM

After the Quantity is entered the Item selection box will appear. Select the Item you wish to select or left mouse click. If you have a touch screen touch the name of the item.

Sub Items and Forced Up Charges

- Note that if the buttons are disabled Follow Metro needs you to select the forced upcharge prior to moving forward. The Message in Yellow under the quantity buttons will display the item that was selected. After you select the forced upcharge (sometimes called sub item) then the buttons will enable again.

Selecting the Forced Upcharge. If you have created forced upcharges in the Utilities – Item Management. The Upcharge list will appear after you select the item. This is a forced upcharge and your counter people will be FORCED to select one of the options on the list. They are only allowed to select one of the options. This is for types of items. I.e. Coats: Regular, Long, short, Rain coat. This is not an optional upcharge. For those use the optional upcharge option.

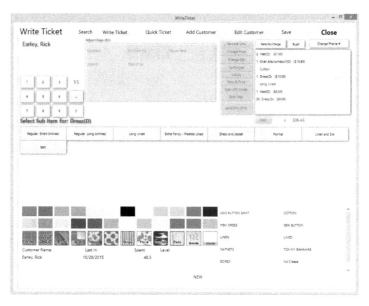

Optional Up Charges

If you have a large screen then the optional upcharges will appear on the bottom right. (This option can also be turned off in the store manager window. The system will also list all the optional upcharges connected to the class selected by pressing the Upcharge button after selecting the item and/or forced upcharge. To select the quantity of the optional upcharge press the quantity button prior to selecting the upcharge listed.

Colors

Color buttons are also located on the bottom of the Write ticket window. You must select the color after you have selected an item and forced upcharge if they exist for the selected item. You can add quantities to the color by selecting the quantity button prior to selecting the color.

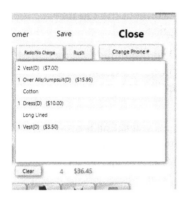

The class code will appear after each item and the price multiplied by the Quantity will appear after the item description.

Buttons

Remove Line – To remove a line item select the Item that has been entered from the Item listing with the touch screen or left mouse button. Then press the Remove Line button. You can not remove the upcharge without removing the item first.

Change Price – To change the unit price of an item select the item on the list on the right then press the Change Price button. A popup will appear, enter the new unit price, then press OK, The item will be updated with the unit price equal to the Quantity multiplied by the new unit price.

Change Qty – To change the quantity of items select the item on the right then press the Change Qty button. Enter the new Quantity and the new price will be displayed.

Upcharges and Colors button will list all the upcharges and colors in the item window area. Selecting the option will assign the upcharge or color to the last item selected.

Desc & Price – This option will allow you to enter a description and a custom price. This is used for items that are not on the list.

Scan Codes – This button is used to scan barcodes such as UPC codes on items you sell in the store.

Saving and Printing Tickets

To Save and Print – Press the button on Save/Print
(F10) . A Calendar will appear to select the Pickup or
Delivery Date. It will default to the Default days to
pickup stored in the Store Manager Window.

Print Window

Print Winow –The last window before saving allows you to enter Prepayments, Deposits, Garments Tag numbers (if using manual tags) and select the type of print. To just print the tickets and optional tags press the buttom right Print Ticket button. For Direct sales (items are the ticket are being picked up now, press the Direct Sale Button)

Coupons can be selected from the coupon list (to add coupons go to Utilites – Coupon Manager)

X – the x buttons will remove tax or prepayments if in error.

Emailing Tickets

To use the email system there are several step to setup the email

(We recommend that you call the Follow Support 760.282.4421 and setup an appointment for a tech to install your client)

1. Enter the SMTP information for your email provider

2. Use the Internal Email option unless you have previously setup the Blat program.

3. Enter email addresses for your customers.

4. If the customer selected has an email account the Ticket and pickup reminders will automatically be sent.

Prepayments

To use Prepayments on tickets, simply press the Prepayment button on the final Ticket window. Enter the prepayment amount (either the full amount of the ticket or partial amount) in the tendered amount then press the payment type. For Cash press cash, check press check. To place the amount on account press the On Account button (You do need to allow the customer to be on account before this button is enabled)

** To allow a customer place tickets on account go to the customer window, then the Accounts Tab and place a check in the "Account Customer" then save. This will enable the Place on Account option on prepayments and ticket pickup and allow the customer to be visible in the Account Window.

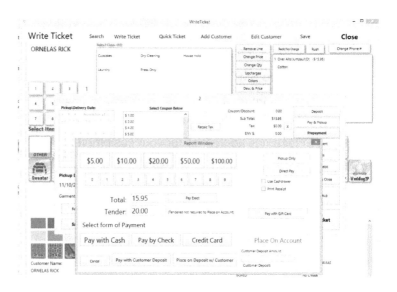

** Place on Deposit w/ Customer is different than a prepayment. The deposit is a set amount of cash that is placed on deposit with the customer to be used optionally on any ticket in the system. The prepayment is a prepaid amount of cash assigned only to this ticket. To Enter a deposit (ie for Leather) press the place on deposit w/ customer button and enter the deposit amount. To use a deposit on a ticket press the pay with customer deposit button and the deposit amount will be subtracted from the deposit and used to pay this ticket.

Direct Pay and Immediate Pickup

Direct Pay is used for items being sold and picked up directly. This is for purchases that are sold over the counter at you store that do not require processing. This could be used for the direct sale of Dresses, Coffee, soap, etc. After the Direct pay button is pressed the Ticket is immediately placed on Status Picked Up.

Inventoried Items

If the items being purchased on this ticket are noted as Inventoried (in the item manager) then the current stock is reduced by the number of items being purchased. Note below that the Current Qty is 55 and the reorder point is 10 as well as a checkbox in the Inventory Item option. With this setting the Current Qty of 55 will be reduced each time this item is purchased. When the Current Qty reaches 0 then the item will no longer appear on the item menu for purchasing.

Loyalty Points

Loyalty System – Follow has several forms of Loyalty. The most common form is the Loyalty with cash rewards based on dollar levels. To set up loyalty go to the Store manager and select the Loyalty Program tab. Then Turn on the check box next to Use Loyalty Program.

To use Loyalty by the total dollar sales of each customer place a check next to the "Set Loyalty by $ Value of Ticket" The set the Loyalty Level to reach for reward to the dollar value the customer must achieve before they receive the "Reward Bonus Dollars"

** Then As the customer reaches the total sales in the loyalty level then will automatically receive the Reward Bonus Dollars in their House account. You can view and modify Reward dollars for each customer in the Customer Edit window under sales.

To reward customer bonus dollars based on total number of Tickets then turn off the "Set Loyalty by $ Value of Ticket" and turn on the "Set Loyalty by # of Tickets"

Coupons

To create coupons to be available in the Ticket Window. Enter the Utilities Top menu and select the Coupon manager. Then select the coupon you wish to modify or press Add Coupon to add a new coupon not in the List. The Coupon Description can be anything that describes the coupon clearly. Then to enter a % coupon enter the % in the Coupon % amount field. Then enter the Class codes in the Applicable Classes field. This Class Code is critical. If the user enters only Laundry Items and your coupon is only for D (meaning Dry cleaning) then no amount will be taken off the ticket. Enter all the Class codes that you wish the coupon to apply to.

Describe and Price Items

To enter a customer item and price select the Desc & Price item in the item list. If the Desc & Price item is not available then add an item to the class in the Item manager with code 0 (zero) (code 0 is reserved for Desc & Price in each class) and indicate that it is a Desc & Price Item.

Then select the item, enter a description then enter a price. After pressing OK the Item description and custom price will appear on the Ticket.

Laundry Wash & Fold

To enter Wash & Fold you need to set an item up with the option "Enter Quantity" turned on. In the Item Management Window found under the Utilities menu. Select the Laundry class, then select or Add the item Wash & Fold. Enter the Price as the unit price per unit (usually pounds) then select the "Enter Quantity" checkbox, and enter a unique code and enter the Description as Wash & Fold. (see image below)

To enter Wash & Fold items on a ticket, select the Laundry Class and click on Wash & Fold in the Item area. Then enter the number of pounds or units then press OK.

If you wish to use other units of measure then enter the unit description in the item edit window under Quantity Label. (ie Kilos etc)

Alterations and Piece Count

To enter Alteration items, first make sure you have an Alteration Class added under Class management.

Then enter the Item manager and select the Alteration class from the drop down class box. Then either select an alteration item to change or press the Add an Item button to add a new item.

Enter the following required information:

Code – A unique code from the alteration list. This is usually a single letter or number (you can use multiple letters or numbers but for keyboard entry you want to use single letters or numbers. Touch screen or mouse entry doesn't require single letters or numbers)

Item Description – Enter the description of the Alteration.

Pieces – Use this for alterations not included with a cleaning. So if the item were to be altered and not cleaned at the same time and you need to include in the piece count and or tag printing then you need to enter a piece count. Example: For a blouse being sewn you would enter pieces 1 but for a 2 pc suit being sewn then you would enter 2. If the Item is included in a cleaning then the piece is automatically not added.

Alteration Type – Select this option for all alterations so Follow can ask the user if the alteration is attached to a dry cleaning or laundered item to include or not include in the piece count.

Forced upcharges or sub items can be added if required.

Correcting Mistakes

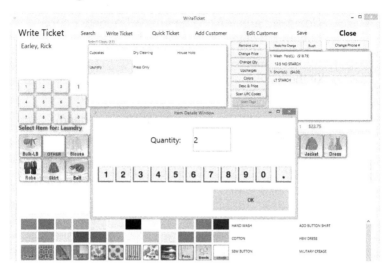

On both the Write Ticket and Edit Ticket Windows there are Correction buttons. Each button will change the item line selected.

To change quantity – If you enter 1 item and wish to change the quantity on line to 2, select the line, press the "Change Qty" button, enter the new quantity to 2 then press OK.

To change the price select the line, press the "Change Price" button, enter the new price then press ok..

Remove line will delete the selected line.

To Change the status on the Ticket press the Change Status until the desired status appears.

To Void the Ticket, simply Edit the Ticket and press the Void button.

Messages

To add private messages for or about customer enter the Customer Manager and enter a Message in the Comment area. All comments will appear on the bottom left of the Write,Edit and Pickup Ticket Windows.

(If the comment does not display – You may wish to upgrade your monitor to a higher resolution screen)

Min. Resolution screens do not display bottom portions.

Entering Manual Garment Tags

Garment tags can be automatically printed or no. If you choose to use the Espon U220 or Star SP 700 and print garment tags for the clothes then each tag will include the ticket number, customer name and due date of the item. During assembly you simply match the ticket number on the tag with the ticket number on the ticket.

If you choose to use non computer printed tags then you have 6 spaces on the Final Print Ticket Window where you can enter each tag range. Usually you will only need 1 such as GRN-01-05 or you can enter a different range for Dry cleaning and another tag range for Laundry.

During assembly you match the tag on the clothes with the extra tag stapled to the ticket.

If an item of clothing is found and needs to be matched to a ticket you can select the Garment manager and search the tag directly.

This window can also be used to assign the tag during the marking stage to tickets already created.

Automatic Garment Tag System

To turn on the Automatic Tag system to print custom garment tags that are stapled to the garments. First

Turn on the Print tags with ticket option found in the store manager under the Ticket tab. After the option is turned on then plug in and install the windows driver for either the Epson U220 or the Star SP700.

Then the batch file on the client will need to be modified to direct the tag to the proper printer.

The batch file is located in the Follow Directory and called: prttag.bat

The batch file is an ascii file that includes the following lines

The file includes the Type command with the TAG.TXT file name. Then the > greater than sign directing the file to the computer name and printer share name. ie.

Type TAG.TXT > \\FollowSamsung\TAG

Scanning Bar Codes and Clothes Tags

The Follow Metro has 2 types of Scanning available for store owners. You can assign UPC or barcode tag numbers to any item. Then when you write a ticket press the SCAN button and scan the tag with the barcode reader. The item will automatically be added to the ticket and priced.

The second use for the scan tags is to assign preprinted barcode tags to articles of clothing. Then press (using the thermopath system available at cleanersupply.com) the tag onto the garment. When the user brings the item back to the store you press the scan button then scan the barcode and the item is added to the ticket.

If you assign tags to Item such as lint brushes or other inventoried items then you enter the item management area and scan the barcode of the item into the Stock number field. Then enter the current inventory quantity in the "Current Qty" field. Then enter a reorder point. Then check the Inventory Item check box. When this item is selected in the write ticket window then a unit is removed from current qty. Letting you know how many are left in inventory at any time

Printing Tickets

To print the Ticket press the Print and Save Ticket button. On this final confirmation window you can enter the Garment Tag (if you are not using the automatic Garment Tag printer), the days to Pick up (This is a default in Ticket Properties. You can change it there) Change the number of pieces. Enter the Coupon or a Discount (If the customer has a Discount in the Customer file this will automatically appear (But you must have created a % discount in Utilities – Coupon Management for that type of percentage)

If the customer is purchasing a Cash Sale item only, such as a lint brush you want to press the Cash Sale (F9) button. This will allow you to enter the cash now and will not place this ticket into the production system by marking the ticket Picked Up immediately. The ticket will be marked Picked Up today and the sale will be added to the cash drawer.

The deposit button allows you to enter money onto the ticket that will be credited when the ticket is picked up. This can be used for leather or alterations that you do not know the exact price.

To Preview the ticket, click the Preview checkbox, then press the print button. If you have a separate tag printer and you have turned on the Print tags with tickets the Tags check box will be checked and tags will print when you press print. To stop the tags from printing uncheck the box. To only print the tags for the ticket or reprint the tags press the Print Tags button. To save the information but close this Ticket without printing press the close button.

Printing Tags

See: **Automatic Garment Tag System**

Ticket Deposits

The Final print page after Writing a Ticket or Editing a Ticket include a Deposit button on the top right of the window. This button will allow you to enter a deposit amount for items on the ticket. This is not a prepayment. The deposit will be placed on the customer file and will be available to use to pay for the ticket or return to the customer during the pickup process.

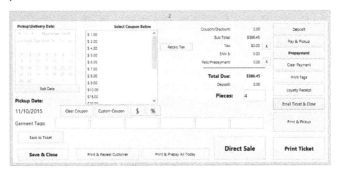

In the pickup window if the customer has money on deposit you can press the button "Pay with Customer Deposit". This action will check if a deposit is available and will use that amount to pay for the tickets selected. If the deposit is more than the due amount then the remaining balance will be put back into the customer deposit.

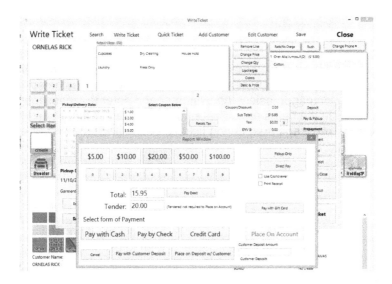

Selecting a New Class for the Item List

SELECTING A NEW CLASS – PRESS THE CLASS BUTTON

Changing the Class can be done by selecting the **Class** button at the bottom of the screen or pressing **F12** in the Quantity Field. You can also turn on auto pop up class option in the Ticket Properties. You can choose to have the class option window appear at the beginning of each ticket or at the beginning of each item.

There are also quick class buttons that appear at the bottom of the screen. Just press one of these buttons.
The M and L buttons can be used for Men's or Ladies classes. (The C Class is a Consignment button for Consignment Inventoried Items.)

Customer Message

To enter a message for the customer or to the counter person about the customer, then enter the customer manager, select the customer and enter the message in the notes are. These notes will appear the message area during ticket creation and pickup.

Cancel the Ticket

When creating or editing a ticket if you wish to cancel the ticket simply use the back arrow in the upper left corner to cancel and not save the ticket. If you have already saved the ticket and wish to cancel, then select the edit manager, select the ticket then press the Void button.

Quick Ticket

Quick Tickets are used in busy stores or used during busy periods. As the customer drops off their clothes you would select the customer by highlighting the customer name then press the Quick Ticket button on the left menu. Then enter the number of garments and press the save and print. Then select the pickup date and print. The ticket will print with just basic information and the number of pieces but no itemization of the items. At another station or at a later time you would select edit ticket, enter the ticket number from the quick ticket, then itemize the ticket and reprint.

Picking Up Tickets

- To pick up tickets, press the **Pick up (F3)** button from the Main Menu
- When picking up a ticket:
  1. Select the customer by entering the customer account number or double click on the account in the look up window.
  2. Select the tickets from the list of the tickets that the customer wishes to pickup. Click on the item check box and a check will indicate that the ticket has been selected. To unselect an item click again. To select all the tickets press the Select all button or press [F5]. Notice the amount change in the Total selected box.
  3. Once the tickets have been selected, press the **Cash Out** button. The types of payment available for this customer will appear in the **Type of Payment** window. Press the **Select Payment Type** button to select the preferred method of payment.

Selecting Customers

First select the customer.

To Search for a Customer enter the customer's phone number or name (or part of a name) in the "Enter the Search Information" field at the top of the screen. Once the Grid highlights the Customer's information then press Enter to Select the Customer.

(You can select a customer by pressing Enter when the customer is highlighted, or double click on the customer or click the Select and Close button at the bottom of the screen)

To Pick up a Ticket by Ticket Number press the "By Ticket no (F3)" button after you have scanned the number in the field above or entered the ticket number then press F3 or click the By Ticket No. button.

Viewing Ticket Items

Select the tickets from the list of the tickets that the customer wishes to pick up. Click on the item check box and a check will indicate that the ticket has been selected. To unselect an item click again. To select all the tickets press the Select all button or press [F5]. Notice the amount due changes in the Total selected box area.

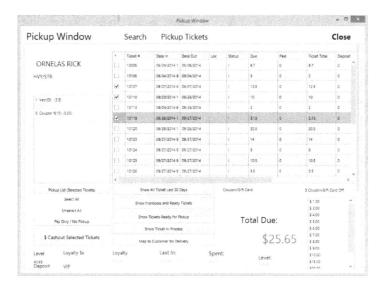

Once the tickets have been selected, press the **Cash Out (F10)** button. The types of payment available for this customer will appear in the **Type of Payment** window. Press the **Select Payment Type** button to select the preferred method of payment.

Notice the Display Orders that are: Ready for Pickup. If a customer has a question on a Ticket that does not appear to be on the list of Tickets Ready for Pickup you can select a different status and view the Picked up tickets or the Tickets "In Process" to let the customer know when the ticket will be ready or when they picked up the order.

Editing Tickets

If you need to modify a ticket to redo an item or change a price or quantity, then return to the main menu and press the Edit Ticket button, select the Ticket then make the change and save. You can select tickets by entering the ticket number, customer account number or enter a date range and view all the tickets written during that period. After searching for ticket select the ticket then press the "Edit Ticket" button.

Once you are on the Edit ticket window. Select the item on the right then press the action button to the left of the item list.

Selecting Multiple Tickets for Pickup

To select several tickets for pickup simply left mouse click or touch the ticket numbers. A check box will appear to the left of the ticket number indicating the ticket is selected for pickup.

Cashing Out

The types of payment available for this customer will appear in the **Type of Payment** window. Press the **Select Payment Type** button to select the preferred method of payment.

Notice the Display Orders that are: Ready for Pickup. If a customer has a question on a Ticket that does not appear to be on the list of Tickets Ready for Pickup you can select a different status and view the Picked up tickets or the Tickets In Process to let the customer know when the ticket will be ready or when they picked up the order.

Printing Receipts

To set up receipts you need to first setup the receipt option in the Store manager indicating under the Printers tab which printer will print the receipt.

After a Credit card is processed 2 copies of a Credit Card receipt will print. 1 for the Customer and one for the Merchant.

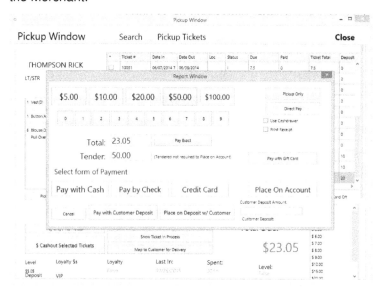

If the customer wishes a receipt along with their copy of the ticket then you can also select the Print Receipt checkbox located on each cash out window. This window appears after you cash out in the pickup window and prepayment window.

PROCESSING CREDIT CARDS AND CASHING OUT

After pressing the Cash Out [F10] key or clicking on the button the Cash out window will appear for Pay by Cash Pickups

If you wish to pay by Credit Card the Credit card must be entered into the Credit Card field in the Customer Window.

To pay by Credit Card select the Pay by Credit card check box and press the cash out button. The following message will appear.

If you would like to enter a new credit card for this transaction, select "**No**".

** If you have enrolled with x-charge.com for automatic credit card processing then the swipe card window will appear.
Just swipe the card and press ok. If the card is decline Follow will inform you that the card is declined and ask the user to enter another form of payment. If the card is authorized then the auth # will be placed into the cash drawer and the tickets will be automatically paid.

X-charge.com has offered the x-charge software ($500 per station) free for any Follow user with a month to month contract and special very low rates. Follow only uses the x-charge company due to this unbelievable deal.

To setup integrated credit card processing call x-charge

- Credit Card Processing

  Integrated with Follow X-CHARGE

  1202 High Tech Circle Henderson, Nevada

  89015

  www.Acceleratedpay.com

- (800) 637-8268 x111
  Fax:(702) 446-8145
  philip.head@acceleratedpay.com

Paying by Check

If you select to Pay by Check the check window will appear:

Enter the Check information than press ENTER or click on the Close button. The Cashout Window will than appear. Enter the check amount into the Cash Tendered Field.

Editing Tickets

Searching for Tickets

To modify tickets that have already been created, simply select the Edit Ticket Option from the main menu. Then select the form of search and search for the ticket you wish to change.

The search window includes search for ticket within a date range or searching by account number (phone) , name or ticket number. Enter the search criteria then press the search button. After the ticket appears in the search results, select the ticket line then press the Edit button on the left.

Voiding Tickets

To void the ticket select the ticket line in the search result then press the Void Ticket button.

Changing Items

To change, remove or modify the items on a Ticket select the ticket, press the Edit button, then use the change buttons on the right side of the window.

To use the change buttons, select the line you wish to change on the Ticket Item list of items on the far right of the screen, then press the button to make the type of change you wish.

Reprinting Tickets

To Reprint a ticket, Enter the Edit Ticket Window, search for the ticket, then press the Edit Ticket button located on the left menu panel.

To reprint from the Edit Window after selecting the ticket, press Print and Save button on the right button panel area.

View Ticket History

Edit Ticket history can be viewed by pressing the Information button on the Button Panel. You can also view the Ticket history by pressing the Ticket History button from the Edit Ticket search window by pressing the Ticket History link.

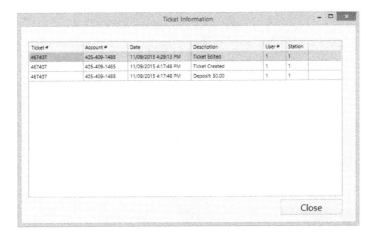

Partial Payments

Follow support different forms of partial payments. The most common is to pay less than the total value of the tickets selected in the pickup window. Follow will continue to keep the ticket on the pickup window for the customer until the full amount is payment. The location of the ticket will indicated "Customer" but the status will show in process reminding the counter person that the customer has not fully paid. You also have other options, the customer can be modified to be allowed on account. This will allow the counter

person to select the On Account button on the
payment window for any ticket for this customer.
Then the Ticket can be transferred to the Accounts
Receivable module. The AR Module will allow you to
send Statements to these customers and allow the
customer to pay on time.

Removing Items

After selecting the Ticket from the Edit search
window, select the item in the item list in the upper left
corner of the screen. Then press the Remove Item
button. After removing an item make sure to save and
print to recalculate the value of the ticket.

Changing Status

The Follow system using status and location to keep
track of Tickets with in the System and your
production environment. The following status' are
available and will change automatically as you
process the items.

1. Q – Quick Ticket – When a Quick Ticket is create
and no items are added to the Ticket.

2. I - In Process – This is the status an item has when
the ticket is created and itemized

3. R – Ready – The Ticket has been assigned a location after cleaning or has been marked ready.

4. V – Voided – The Ticket has been voided and will not be included in the sales reports

5. P – Pickup Up – The Ticket has been Picked up by the customer

6. D – Delivered – The Ticket has been Delivered through the Delivery module.

If you wish to change the status manually Select the ticket in the Edit Ticket Search window and press the Change Status until the desired status appears then save.

Ticket Options

By pressing the **Ticket Options** or **F8** button at the top right of the **Edit Ticket** screen you can enter additional information about a ticket. This would normally be used for editing tickets and viewing additional information or for modifying the information before printing the Ticket.

Garment tag numbers and prepayment information as well as the pickup date can be entered after you press the print button on the final print window. The status is defaulted from the Configuration setup. When a ticket is entered it is in Process, after it is marked ready it is automatically changed to "Ready" (Unless you press the Send to Alteration or Send to Plant buttons). The final status after it is "Picked up" will be "P" for Picked Up or "V" for Voided or "D" for Delivered.

Price Lookup

To check prices of an item you can press the Price Lookup button from the main menu. Select the Class and view the item prices.

Customer History

The Customer Reports include the Customer Ticket Listing Summary Report. This report is available from the Reports top menu under the Customer Reports option. Select the Customer History Report from that menu.

You will be asked to select a customer from a customer search window and a date range for the ticket in date.

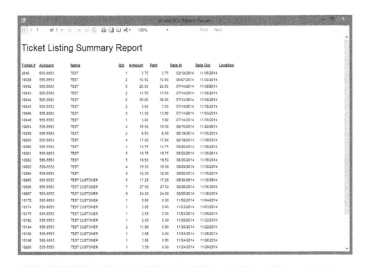

Assign Locations

To Assign locations press the F10 function key from the main menu. Then scan the ticket, then the location. When you are done press the F12 key to exit. The Assign Location screen will display all other orders and their location in the box below, this is so you can place the order near the other Orders. If you have a Bar Code scanner and Bar Codes on the Racks (there is a report for this under Reports) and on the ticket you can scan the Ticket then Scan the new location.

Mark Tickets Ready

To change the status of a Ticket in the production cycle select the Mark Ticket Ready button from the main menu. After the Window appears type or scan the barcode on the tickets. After scanning the ticket the system will change the status of the ticket scanned to "R" (Marking the Ticket Ready). If the auto email system is turned on then the system will email the owner of the ticket that their Clothes are ready for pickup. If the option to Assign to Plant or Assign to Alteration is checked then the status will remain "I" In process.

*The send Delivery email option will send an email to the user that the clothes are ready for email.

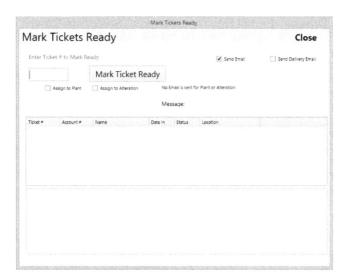

Time Card System

The time card system is a third party system that is opened when the Time Card menu option is selected. The demo is included with the Follow 8 system and will support 1 employee. To purchase this module you can pay 21.95 at the www.econsoft.com site for unlimited employees.

X-Charge Credit Card Processing

See X-Charge Application – Credit Card Processing

End of Day Report

End of day can be run at the change of a shift or at the end of the day. To run the report select the Cash

Drawer , End of Day report button. Select the Cash
drawer # and the Date Out, then press the End of Day
Report button.

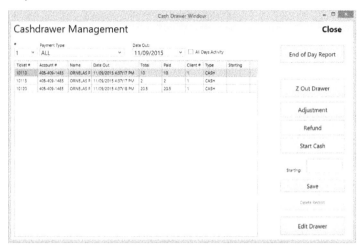

After the report is run you can Z Out the drawer by
pressing the Z Out Drawer button. This will clear out
the drawer for the day marking the orders Z'd out.

Adjustments can also be made to any drawer by
pressing the Adjustment button and entering an
amount to be adjusted. If you needed to remove
$10.00 from the drawer you would make a drawer
adjustment of -10.00

To change a $ amount of any Ticket picked up select
the Edit drawer button and modify the line then press
Save Changes.

To remove any transaction from the list, select the row
and press the Delete Record button.

After you Z out the drawer for a day or shift, then
press the Start Cash button and enter the total dollar
amount of the Starting Cash for the following day or
shift.

Outside Processing

To use the outside processing functions to keep track of tickets outside the plant use the assign location option.

Once you select a Ticket you can type in the name or number of a location or press the assign to plant or assign to alteration button. These two buttons will mark the location of the item to the plant or alteration without assigning the status to "Ready" keeping the status to In Process.

Globally Replace Account Numbers

Most cleaners use the phone number for account numbers. This approach creates a problem when a customer moves or changes their phone number. When this occurs you may do one of several things. Create a new customer under the new account or globally replace the old account number throughout the system with the new one. The **Global Replace Account Number** option is located under the **Customer Manger Window in the Tools tab**.

Press the button to Replace Account Number then enter the new number then press the replace button.

Office Management

Customer Manager

To get to the customer information window, click on the **Customers (F11)** button.

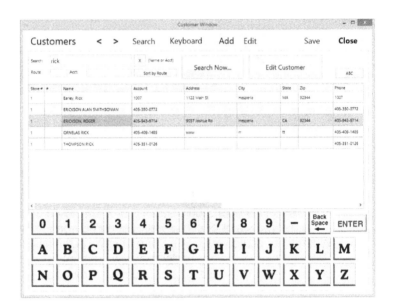

Searching for Customers

SELECTING A CUSTOMER

After selecting add ticket you will be required to select a customer. If the customer is not found or you know they are new press the Add Customer button found in the bottom left area of the Window.

- The default search by is by account number. You may choose to assign account numbers using the automatic account number assignment button "Assign" on the Customer Window or you may choose to assign account numbers as phone numbers (this is most common) or any other numbering naming scheme. You may use characters in the account number as well.

Removing Customers

** To remove a customer follow the instructions below. ** You might just want to set the customer as inactive instead of removing the customer. Removing the customer you lose all the history.

After selecting the customer from the Customer Management Window. Press the Edit Customer button on the left. Then Select the Functions Tab. A button indicating Remove the Selected Customer will be available.

After you press the Remove the Selected Customer button. You will be asked to confirm the Delete of this customer. Press OK to Delete and Cancel not to remove.

Editing Customer Information

- The Route/Delivery Information Tab which includes all the basic information:

- Route – This is used for the Delivery System; allowing you to enter this customer on a given route for printing and processing deliver Manifest. (See Delivery Section later in Manual)

- Stop Number – This is the Stop on the Route, used for ordering this customer on the Manifest

- Hotel Indicator – If you have Hotel's this is used to tell the system that this is a Hotel Customer. When this box is checked and a Ticket is written for this customer the system will prompt you for the Room number and Name of the Guest.

- The Default Class that will allow you set up separate price lists for these customers. This default Class allows you to negotiate different pricing for Hotel or Wholesale customers. Whenever a customer with this default class creates a ticket the default class item list and upcharges will appear.

- Starch Preference – This will appear on the Comment area on the Screen when you select this customer. You can also add the "Comment" field to the ticket to print the starch preference as well.

- Pricing Level – (see the Item Management area) will assign this customer to the Item Price Level you created. Every time this customer has a ticket enter they will receive different prices than others.

- Whole Sale Account – This will allow you to enter a Ticket Number and name from the agency that is associated with this customer. This will allow the billing for this customer to be the Whole sale account and will allow all Tickets entered under this customer to fall under this whole sale account and will track their names

Account information

- The Billing information tab that is used for Accounts receivable billing addresses.

- The Billing Account needs to be the same as the Account number above; if you enter another account number here when this customer places orders on account the billing will be transferred to the new account number.

- This is used for Police, fireman, or families with husband and wife bring orders in separately but you only wish to send one bill

- **% Discount during AR transfer** – This will take a percentage off or add a percentage to the Ticket when transferring to Accounts Receivable. This is used for Hotels when you wish the ticket to show the full price and the bill to be less a percentage (or add a percentage with a negative number) Do not enter a % sign just the number 10 for 10% discount.

- **% Discount** – This will automatically add a discount to the ticket every time the customer adds a ticket. This Discount will show on the Ticket. To enter a discount you need to enter the Manager's password (default is 2164) into the **Enter Password Here then Press Button Below:** section then click the **Submit Password to Open Discount, Account, And Credit Card**. Then select the checkbox to allow this customer to place orders at Pickup on Account.

- The Credit Card Number Field and Exp. Date is used to keep a card number on file for automatic processing from Follow to charge the credit card when the pickup and you select Credit Card. This is also used for billing the Credit Card in a batch for Delivery Customer or at the end of the month for Credit Card Customers who wish to be billed monthly from the Accounts Receivable

- The **Sales Information** tab that allows you to view the Sales Marketing data for this customer, and the **House Account/Tags** is used for customers that wish to place funds on account with your store or for customer's that pick up items without paying the total bill, but do not wish to open an Accounts Receivable account with you.

- The default picture for the Account number can be changed in the main menu properties window. If you do not wish to use the Phone number format make sure to change this.

Cash only Customers

To mark a customer as cash only select the cash only check box on the Customer Manager window. This will disable all the non cash options in the cash windows.

Customer Comments

Customer comments are entered in the customer comment area of the General Tab under the Customer Manager. The Alter check box will popup the comment as an alert anytime a ticket is written or picked up for this customer.

Customer Preferences

You can manually set customer preferences in the comment area or setting the starch preference in the customer Manager General tab. But the starch is also set automatically when you select a starch preference from the Write Ticket Window.

Email Information

To enter customer email information select the customer manager and enter the email under the email field. If the email system has been configured and turned on then the customer will be emailed copies of the ticket as well as pickup reminders automatically.

VIP/Loyalty Customers

Follow has a **Loyalty System** that
● Keeps track of customer total Sales and print automatic Coupons when a customer has reached a level.

- Keeps track of total number of tickets and prints automatic coupons
- Credits the Customer with a Dollar credit that can be redeemed automatically on their next pickup.

To turn on the Loyalty system you must:

- **Loyalty Level by Dollar Amount**: Enter **System Properties** and enter the total dollar amount, in the **Loyalty Information** field, that must be achieved before the coupon is printed. Then enter the **Class Code** of any class that you do not want to be part of the total calculation of Loyalty points. Then select the **Loyalty by $ Total.**
- **Loyalty Level by Order Quantity**: Enter **System Properties** and enter the total number of tickets in the Item field that must be achieved before the coupon is printer. Then enter the **ClassCode** of any class that you do not want to be part of the total calculation of Loyalty points. Then select**Loyalty Points by Order Quantity**.
- If you wish the customer to get **Loyalty Reward Dollars** added to their account when they achieve the level above, enter the dollar amount in the **Loyalty Reward $ (0 for Coupon only),** field.

Loyalty customers must the Loyalty Customer check box checked in the Customer Manager Window.

*For Assistance Technical support will configure the loyalty report for you.

If you choose to turn on the Loyalty Reward Dollars the Dollars will be placed in the Sales Tab of the

Customer Window. To manually add sales dollars or loyalty reward dollars select this tab and add values manually.

Add Customers

Press the **Add Customer** button to open the window to under the Customer Manager or Write Ticket Window.

The window will appear blank in add mode. For a basic customer you will need an **account number** and a **name**. If you use the **Assign** button on the left of the Account you should get the customer's **phone number** and place it in the **phone number** field. If you use phone numbers for account numbers (which is most common) the system will automatically populate the phone number field with the account number you entered as you exit the account number field.

Set Customers to Taxable

To set customers to taxable you must first turn on the "Auto set customers to Taxable" option in the Store Manager window (When this option is on all new customers will be automatically marked as Taxable) or individually turn on the Taxable option in the Customer Manager Edit window.

You also need to set the tax rate in the Store Manager and set the Classes Taxable Under the Class Manager under the Utilities option. The class option allows you to charge tax to some classes and not others. Ie. Charge tax on Dry Cleaning but not Alterations.

Delivery Customers

Delivery customers are marked by assigning a delivery route to the customer in the Customer Manager. Optionally you can also enter stop number. All reports are sorted by stop number.

(It's also critical to set up a form of payment with each delivery customer)

Setup Taxable Customers

If the option to default all new customers to taxable is turned on the new customers will be checked as taxable automatically when added. For non taxable customers you would need to turn off the Taxable option on the customer screen.

Tax rates are set in the Store manager.

Classes can be set to taxable or non taxable in the Class Manager.

Wholesale Accounts

To setup a Wholesale Account, set up the Customer in the **Customers (F11)** window with the address and Billing information. Select the Wholesale Account checkbox in the bottom right of the Billing Information tab.

Then use the **Office – Wholesale Account's** Menu option to enter in the rest of the information such as Discount or parent relationships to other Customers. Each Ticket written will receive the Discount % found on the Billing Information tab. The Wholesale

Discount will be used in the Wholesale statement taking a total % off the total of all orders. It is best to set up a new Class and price list for each wholesale since most wholesale prices are negotiated individually then set the default class on the customer to that class.

Custom Ticket for Customer

Follow has the ability to print special Tickets for Customers that look different than the default ticket. To enter a special ticket you must select the customer, Enter the House Account/Canadian tab and enter the ticket name in the Special Ticket Name field: Make sure the ticket name start with the word "TICKET" in uppercase. Then enter the ticket name after the word TICKET.   An example might be TICKET_HOLIDAYINN. This might be a special ticket designed when a Hotel guest from the Holiday Inn has an order.

Account Manager

To enter the Accounts Receivable Window select the Back Office from the top menu and select Accounts Receivable then select the Accounts Receivable maintenance option. You will be asked to select a customer. Double click on the customer and the customer transactions will appear.

Creating Accounts

The **Accounts Receivable** section of Follow Classic allows your customers to have an account in the system, which can be used to process statements at the end of every month and also process an automatic credit card payment if you wish too. So for example, if you write a ticket, you have the ability to put the customer's bill under that their account.

The first thing you should do is obviously have a customer added onto an account. To do that, enter the **Customer Search Window** from the **Main Menu** and select a customer so that you have the customer's information on screen. Under the **"Billing and Accounting Information"** tab, you will see a check-box that reads **"Allow this Customer to be a Charge Account.'** It may be grayed out so type in the default password, which is **2164**. Once that's done, click the submit button below, allowing you to modify any of the field on the left about the customer. Click Save and Close once you're done.

Remember that you need the Manager's permission if you are using different access levels.
*Also, adding the credit card number allows for automatic credit card processing at the end of each month,
*Only new tickets written will be added to this specific customer's account

From here, you are basically done adding a customer to the accounts module of Follow Classic. You may continue by writing tickets for those who are in the system.

Place Tickets on Account

To place a Ticket on account, select the Pickup Tickets module from the main menu. Select the customer and select the ticket or tickets to be placed on account. Press the Cash out button on the bottom left. Then press the On Account button. The total amount due will be placed on account. These Tickets will be immediately transferred over to the Account System.

Make Payments

To apply a payment, press the **Apply a Payment** button on the Accounts Receivable Window.

When the payment window appears enter the dollar amount and the check or card number for reference. This reference # will appear on the statement. You may also make comments such as credit to account or reference to a coupon or comp.

After the close button is pressed the system will ask if you would like this credit applied to open Invoices? If you select "Yes" the system will apply the amount paid to the oldest tickets first and apply as much as possible to each ticket until the credit is used. If you select No. the system will keep this payment on AR as a standing credit and will reflect as such on the invoice adjusting and current or future debt.

All account customers must have a billing account for the account system to work.

Print Statements

To Print Statements Select the **Accounts Module from the main menu.** Select the Customer then press the Print Statement button on the left or from the Edit Account window press the Print Statement button. These options will print individual statements for the selected customer.

To print all the monthly statements for all the account customer press the Print All Statements from the Accounts Window or from the All AR Statements from the Accounts Receivable Reports menu option under the Reports Menu.

.Account Reports

AR Reports include 3 options

Invoice Listing Report by Day will list all the Tickets and Payment made filter by a date range.

Account Customers will print all the Account Customers in the Store.

All AR Statements will print statements for all the Customers marked as Allow on Account.

View / Edit Account Activity

You may apply payments using the button at the bottom of the screen. Using that screen you may pay using cash, check, or credit. To print this customer's statement, you can use its respective button on the top right of the screen. Remember that statements must be printed using an **8.5 x 11in printer**. You may view any existing payments here as well as the current balance due for the customer.

*Remember that to print the statements for all customer under accounts receivable, you must print on the **last day of month**. If all else fails, make sure you revert the date from the operating system (Windows XP, Vista, 7, or 8) back to the last day of the month.

To watch the video, which this newsletter is based upon and more, visit or YouTube channel using the links provided below or just go straight to the video using this link.

AR Aged Report

You can also select the Aged AR Report and simply press the Preview button with No date: This will list all the Account customers and Total the Aged values.

Options for Accounts

You accounting system can have several option ways of being used. The system can use an End of the Month AR Process that moves the balance forward up to a subtotal each month and removes the details for the Tickets that have been paid for. To turn this on enter Ticket Properties and select the Option to "Use End of Month AR Process". Remember that if a Ticket was paid last month and is no longer open the ticket will not display on the Statement if this option is turned on and YOU RUN THE END OF MONTH PROCESS located in Office – Accounts menu option.

Delivery Manager

The Delivery Module in Follow is comprised of a multi-step process that will allow you to set up routes, stops, delivery schedules for the Home, Hotels, Wholesale customers, etc. The following process will work with all delivery customers.

Route Manager

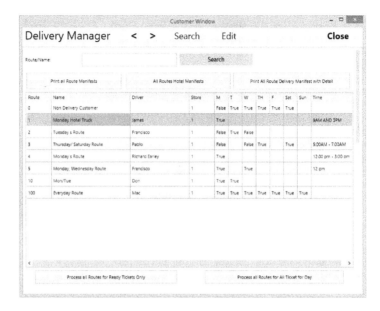

To Create New Routes

Press the Add Button
Then enter a Route name and a Route Number.
Then press the Save Button

** Each route must have a unique number! **

You might call the Routes by the Day of the Week
they deliver or by the Drivers Name and Day of Week.

ie.

JOE - MONDAY or MON/WED ROUTE etc...

Assigning Customers to Routes

Step one of assigning routes is to first create the
routes under the Route Manager on the Main
windows.

To add a new route press the Add Route button then enter a unique route number then a route name. Other information on the Window is optional.

To Assign the Route to the customer select the route from the Route dropdown box in the middle of the Customer Window. If you have ordered your customer by stop number enter the stop number as well. All the delivery and pickup reports will print in stop number order. Then press save.

** Remember you must create the Routes in the Route Manager first.**

Route Pickup Reports

There is a button on the Route manager and the Delivery Manager to Print the Pickup Report. This will print all the pickups for the selected route in stop order. Pickups are Customers that are either on the Regular Route or a Once Pickup. These options are located on the Customer Manager Edit window. To place a customer on a Regular Route, select the route then put a check on the Regular Route check box option. The regular route option indicates that this customer will be picked up each time the driver goes to this route.

The Once option is used for an occasional or one time delivery customer.

Delivery Manifests

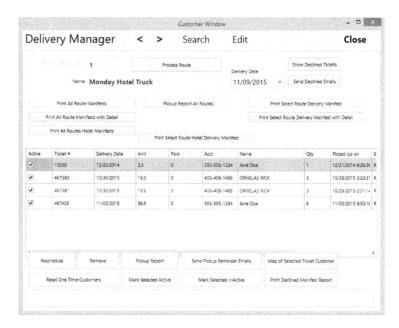

To Print the Delivery Manifest each day for the routes and Tickets scheduled for that day.

1. Select the Delivery Manager from the Main menu, select the route then press the Delivery Manifest button.
2. Select the date of the Delivery.
3. Print the report

You will receive a separate page for each route.

Processing Manifests

The driver takes the Manifest and Signs the bottom after verifying that all the tickets are loaded on the truck.

After each item is delivery he/she will indicate the status after each item. D indicates delivered. Blank indicates that he/she could not delivery the ticket and that ticket is returning to the plant for the next scheduled delivery date.

After delivering tickets, the **Driver** or the **Accounting Person** will enter the Follow System and select **Office – Delivery Management – Manage Delivery Manifest** option from the top menu.

Select the Route on the tree on the left and confirm that the Date is the date you want to process.

By use the right mouse button a popup menu will appear that will allow you to reschedule any ticket that you have currently selected 1,2,3,4,5 or a week later than the current system date. After you select one of the options the ticket will be removed from the list and will not appear again until you select the new date in the date box next to the Process button.

** If you have collected cash, check or a credit card from the customer at the time of delivery you can either user the Pickup module and pay for the ticket directly or process the delivery manifest and transfer the ticket to accounts and make the payment on the Accounts menu. (The advantage of using the Accounts Receivable module is you can always run a statement for the customer at any time to give to the customer showing all Tickets and payments made)

To Process the Manifest and mark all Tickets Delivered and automatically process the payment method, press the Process button.

After Pressing Process the following button will appear to confirm that you want to process this route.

After the Process is complete each ticket will be marked Delivered. All tickets where the customer is marked as "Allow on account" (in the Customer Manager Window) will be immediately transferred to the Account's Receivable module. If the customer is not marked "Allow on Account" but has a Credit card on file, the system will automatically attempt to charge the credit card using the integrated X-charge system. If the Customer has a credit card on file and is marked "Allow on Account" then the ticket will be transferred to the Account's Receivable module but will allow you to batch charge at the end of the period (usually at the end of the month)

- Batch Charge is a process in Account's Receivable that takes all the Tickets for the period and credits adds them up and charges the current balance due to the credit card. If the card and charge is authorized then the payment is automatically applied as a credit to the customers account.

You will note in **Office – Cash Drawer** that the Totals for the tickets in A/R and Credit Cards have included the Tickets for this Route. Also the Edit Ticket Status of this ticket indicates Delivered.

Simple Steps to Setup and Use Delivery

STEP 1:

Setup your routes (routes must not use the number 0 or 99 all other numbers are available) Decide on the route schedule and number the routes based on the truck route and the day or time of delivery. All customers with the same route number will be placed on the same route schedule if a ticket is ready and the date out (scheduled delivery date) is the current date or prior to the current date. (Prior too allows for tickets that were to be delivered on a previous delivery but where not ready to automatically be included in this delivery manifest.)

To Set up the routes select the **Office – Delivery Management – Route Manager (or click the Route Manager option on the main menu)** options from the top menu.

Route 0 is always reserved for General Non Delivery Customers. The default route for counter systems should always be 0. That way all the counter non-delivery customers will not be placed on a delivery manifest

To Add a route press the Add Route button. Remember to assign a route number that is not currently being used. Only one route per number.

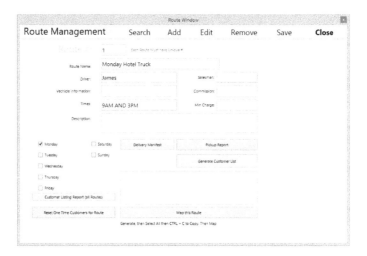

The Required areas are Route number and Route Name. You would normally assign each hotel a separate route number and all tickets written for Employees, Managers, or Hotel Guests would be given a separate Customer under that route all linked to the same route.

Hotels therefor would each have their own Delivery Manifest showing all the rooms and names on each ticket.

Mapping of the Route is available that needs to be done after you have assigned all the customers to the route.

STEP 2:

After the Routes have been added. You need to add the customers under that route by entering the **Customer**s menu and adding each of the customers or reassigning current customer to the newly created routes.

When a customer signs up for your delivery service in the iHomeValet.com site they will be allowed to select one of your routes that you created here. You should be clear in the Route name indicating the Day of the week or area that this route is for. For example: If route 1 is Monday and services North St. Louis. Then the name for route 1 should be "Monday –North St. Louis"

If this customer is a Hotel you will need to place a check in the Hotel checkbox on the Route/ Delivery Information form on the Customer Manager Window. This will inform the add ticket module to Ask the room number and name during the add ticket process and allow you to manage the hotels in the Back Office – Hotel Management – Hotel Management Area.

If the customer charges will be charged to a Credit Card you will want to enter the standing credit card number in the Credit card field under Billing information as well as the Expiration date in MMYY format.

If the customer will be receiving a Statement from you for their charges you will need to indicate that this is an Account customer also under the Billing information tab. Follow will transfer the charge after the delivery manifest has been processed and the ticket has been delivered and the cash drawer has been z'd out for the night.

STEP 3:

Now, Write Tickets for all the Clothes and customer you just picked up.

Usually, you would print a pickup report, then travel to the customer, pickup the clothes and either write the ticket on a laptop or tablet at the location or return to the store and write the tickets in Follow.

STEP 4:

The Ticket is marked ready. This process is critical for delivery. After you have cleaned the clothes you want to use the Mark Ticket Ready module on the main menu. Use the barcode scanner and scan each of the tickets to change the status of the ticket to Ready. (You can default the tickets to Ready when the ticket is added then the delivery system will simply use the dateout as the indicator that the ticket is to be included on the manifest but this becomes difficult to manage.) By using the Mark order ready (and we recommend using bar coded tickets to increase speed and efficiency) you can always be assured that only those tickets ready for delivery will be included in the manifest.

STEP 5:

Now, lets process a ticket for a test customer.

Create a Test Customer and assign the customer in the customer manager to a newly created route.

Print the ticket and process the clothes. Note that the due date on the ticket is 2 days from the date ordered. This ticket will not show up on the manifest for the Monday (Blue Truck route) until the order has been Marked ready and the date is equal or greater than the delivery date you selected when writing the ticket.

(This allows your customers to indicate the exact delivery day to bring the clothes and allows you to indicate the truck closest to that day. On delivery systems it is best to set the days to pick up default in the Store Manage to 1 allowing the tagger/ticket writer to override but this allows the route to determine the schedule.)

STEP 6:

Print the Delivery Manifest each day for the routes for that day.

Enter **Office – Delivery Management** and select the **DeliveryManifest**.

If your Ticket does not appear on the Manifest then check the follow:
1. The Ticket was not marked Ready in the Mark Ticket Ready Module.
2. The customer was not assigned to the Route you selected to print the Manifest for.
3. The Ticket was assigned a Delivery date after the date you selected to print the manifest for. (This feature allows you to pick up and write a ticket for customer who indicates that they are on vacation for a couple of weeks and wants the ticket delivered after they return)

*Note that the **Delivery Date** is set for the **Date Out** schedule of the ticket we entered. The Manifest will list all tickets associated with customers on routes, that are marked ready, and that are scheduled for delivery on or before the Ticket's Delivery Date.*

The driver takes the Manifest and Signs the bottom after verifying that all the tickets are loaded on the truck.

After each item is delivery he/she will indicate the status after each item. D indicates delivered. Blank indicates that he/she could not delivery the ticket and that ticket is returning to the plant for the next scheduled delivery date.

After delivering tickets, the **Driver** or the **Accounting Person** will enter the Follow System and select **Office – Delivery Management – Manage Delivery Manifest** option from the top menu and process the Manifest for each Route that has been delivered.

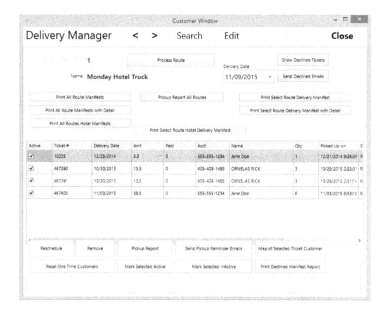

Select the Route on the Grid, select View Ticket and confirm that the Tickets are all delivered that are displayed. (You can change the Date on the top of the window to show Ticket and Manifests from previous or future days).

Once the list only lists those tickets that have been delivered then press the Process button.

After Pressing Process the following button will appear to confirm that you want to process this route.

All Tickets will be marked Delivered and the Customers marked as Allow on Account Tickets will be automatically transferred to the Accounts Receivable Module.

Inventory Manager

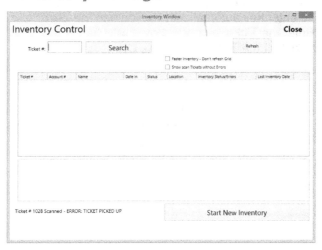

You can use the Inventory Control Module by entering by hand the Ticket number or as I strongly recommend using a bar code scanner. You will first need to include the barcode on the Tickets. This can be done by modify the Ticket so the Ticket number on the top uses the Code 39 Bar code font. This font is located on the Follow CD or you can get this font free from the Internet by searching for Code 39 Font. Follow the Windows instructions for loading new fonts. Then change the font of the Ticket number using the Report writer to Code 39. For assistance Call Follow Tech Support.

Once the Tickets include the barcode ticket number begin your inventory by selecting **Office – Inventory Control**

To begin a new inventory press the "Start Inventory" Button. This will clear the previous inventory and start a new Inventory set.

Doing Inventory

After you scan a Ticket the barcode scanner will press the enter key automatically for you and the Text "Enter the Ticket number above" will change to indicate if the Ticket Number is OK.

If a Ticket is found that has been Picked up, Delivered, Voided or is not currently in the System this Ticket number and the message indicating the problem will appear in the Window. Only those Tickets with problems will appear. To Print or save the List off issues press the View/Print Button.

After you press the **View/Print** button you can select **File – Save** or **File – Print**.

Inventory Reports

This report will appear in Notepad and you can choose to save, email or print.

After the inventory is done make sure to save or print. When a new inventory starts this report will not be available.

Cash Drawer Manager

To get to the cash drawer window click the **Cash Drawer** button or choose **Cash Drawer** from the **Office** tab in the home menu.

Entering Starting Cash

Enter the starting cash in the **Amount** section then press the **Update and Save Amount to Cash Drawer** button.

Audit Drawer

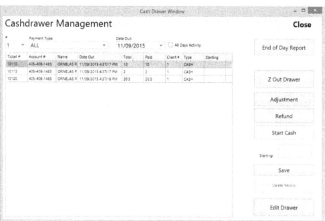

Adjustments to the drawer can be made by selecting the Cash Drawer option from the main menu. Press the Adjustment button, enter the adjustment amount in the Field marked Adjustment, then press the Save Changes button.

Drawer Adjustments

To make adjustments to other drawers select the drawer number, then press the adjustment button, enter the adjustment amount, then press Save Changes.

Multiple Drawer Stores

To manage multiple drawers, enter the drawer number in the configuration area then print drawer reports, enter starting cash, and adjustments by selecting the drawer number on the top of the Cash Drawer Window.

End of Day Report

To run the End of Day report select the End of Day button from the main menu. Select the drawer number then press the End of Day report button.

Cash Drawer Detail Reports

To print a detailed Reconciliation Report listing each ticket sorted and Grouped by Type of Payment: Right mouse click on the Cash drawer Window and Select Cash Drawer Reconciliation Report. Then Press Preview.

Editing the Drawer

To Edit the Drawer press the Edit Drawer button on the top right.

Then enter the manager's password with a level 9 access. (See user manager)

If you wish to not limit the edit drawer to level 9 that option is located under system properties to allow any user level access to the edit drawer function.

Z Out and Clear the Drawer

After printing the reconciliation report press the **Cash drawer Z Out** button to close the drawer.

To update the **Starting Cash** press the **Starting Cash** button.

Email Marketing Manager

Follow includes email marketing modules such as New customer welcome emails, overdue Ticket pickup reminders, missing customer emails, and export to Mail Chimp and email newsletter customers.

These modules are found under the Main Office menu. Each module includes template emails prewritten but allow the user to change the email prior to sending.

To export the emails to other system, select the Export Emails option then press the Export All Customer Emails then copy the emails to the other systems, by selecting all the emails and right mouse clicking and selecting the copy option.

Ticket History

Ticket is available in many different area of Follow. The most common is found in the Ticket Edit area.

After selecting the Ticket in Edit Ticket press the Information button. The transaction history showing all activity on a Ticket is displayed with the user ID and Date and Time of the transaction.

Loyalty Programs

Under the **Loyalty Information** section (that looks like this screen above), you will find several check boxes and text fields assigned for the loyalty system. We'll break it up into steps for you to have an understanding of how to work it to your needs.

Step 1: Loyalty Level
Using the text field provided called the **"loyalty level (by $ or quantity amount)"**, you can enter the amount the customer will need to meet before they can be rewarded by loyalty dollars.

Step 2: Loyalty by Order or $
If you are going to be measuring the loyalty points by either quantity or dollar amount, then you must indicate it by using the check marks provided (on the right). You cannot check on both boxes at once since it will confuse the system, so please be careful. You can also enter the class code and item code using their respective fields. If you don't remember what the class codes are, visit the **Class Management** window to check the keyboard codes.

Step 3: Loyalty Reward $
You can reward customers with loyalty points by giving them either dollar amounts or coupons. Using the field provided called **"Loyalty Reward $ (0 for Coupon only)"**, you can enter the amount. **Ex:** For every $100 they spent with you, then they will receive 10 dollars in reward dollars.

The next step after configuring the loyalty system settings would be to add customers to the loyalty program. To do that, we would need to access a customer's information window from the **Customer** button on the main menu. Under the **Route/Delivery Information** tab, there is a button on the lower left called **Loyalty Program**. To add the customer to the loyalty, simply click the button and they are automatically assigned to the system. If you choose to turn on the loyalty reward dollars, the dollars will be placed in the **House Account** tab of the **Customer** window in the due field as a negative dollar amount. You can change this or remove the amount at any time.

From here, you would need to write tickets for points to be added to their account. You can check their loyalty points by going to **Sales Information** tab under their **Customer Information** window.

Loyalty Report Customization: If you need to customize your loyalty report/ ticket, technical support may do that. You can customize your reports using the Report Builder 2.0 application and Editing the report Called Ticket. All the reports have the *.rdl filename.

To watch the video, which this newsletter is based upon and more, visit our YouTube channel using the links provided below or just go straight to the video using this link.

Coupons and Specials

Coupons can be added and modified using the Utilities top menu and selecting the Coupon Manager. There are 2 types of Coupons: Dollar value coupons and Percent coupons. To Enter the dollar coupons enter the value for the dollar off in the $ Amount Off column. To enter a new percent coupon enter the value in the % coupon amount column.

Each coupon must have the Applicable class codes filled in. If the coupon is only for Dry Cleaning then enter a D in that field. If the coupon is valid for all Laundry and Dry Cleaning then enter a DL for both codes.

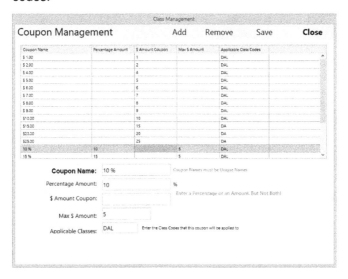

Wholesale Manager

To setup a Wholesale Account, set up the Customer in the **Customers (F11)** window with the address and Billing information. Select the Wholesale Account checkbox in the bottom right of the Billing Information tab.

Then use the **Office – Wholesale Account** Menu option to enter in the rest of the information such as Discount or parent relationships to other Customers. Each Ticket written will receive the Discount % found on the Billing Information tab. The Wholesale Discount will be used in the Wholesale statement taking a total % off the total of all orders. It is best to set up a new Class and price list for each wholesale since most wholesale prices are negotiated individually then set the default class on the customer to that class.

Hotel Valet

Follow includes a Hotel Valet management module to manage Hotel deliveries. This module allows you to create customers who are specific Hotels. Each Hotel will allow you select the hotel during the add ticket process then request the counter person to enter the room number and name of the person in the Room.

Each Hotel should be connected to a special route for the hotel. This will allow you to run delivery manifest specific for each hotel. Billing for the Hotel can be connected directly to the Accounts Receivable to allow you create a billing statement.

Enterprise Store Manager

Store manager is used to modify and manage the store and application configuration information, as well as manage the basic store information used for Ticket and Statement headers. (Store name, address, phone numbers , etc)

Store manager is also used to manage current ticket numbers, tax rates, etc.

Store manager is divided into multiple areas of management. Each of these areas are located in tabs at the bottom.

General – General application settings.

History – This tab allows you to view transactions that have occurred in the application.

Ticket Settings – General Settings for modifying the how the Ticket Application behaves.

Loyalty Program – This tab allows you configure the loyalty program.

Email Settings – This tab allows you set the email smtp settings for configuring the email system.

Tools- This tab allows you to import data from other systems.

Delivery Zip Codes – This tab allows you enter the zip codes that the online website will display your store as delivering to.

Printers – Set printer configurations here.

Language – This tab allows you to change the menu names to your language.

Lot – This tab allows you to configure the Lot system.

Setup Tax Rate

Enter the Tax Rate for the Store Number. This might be a good time to update your store information, addresses and Enterprise relationships. The tree on the left will build as you add your plants, dry stores, etc... You may wish to consider setting up delivery routes and separate sub stores to your plants.

Process Credit Cards

Credit cards can be processed in Follow through the integrated credit card system. To use the integrated system call x-charge

Credit Card Processing
Credit Card Processing through Follow X-CHARGE
Philip Head - 1202 High Tech Circle Henderson, Nevada 89015
www.Acceleratedpay.com
(800) 637-8268 x111
Fax:(702) 446-8145
philip.head@acceleratedpay.com

Batch Processing

(Future Enhancement)

To get to the **Batch Out** menu select the **Office** Tab then select **Batching Out** from the drop menu. Follow will allow you to Batch out many tickets using the barcode reader or entering by hand. This can be if things get busy or if you prefer not to use the cash drawer/Pickup modules. This works great for wholesale tickets as well. Basically you enter the ticket numbers regardless of the customer then cash out all at once. Make sure the tickets are entered in groups and cashed out in groups according to payment type. To batch out select the Pickup by Ticket No. (F9) from the left menu or press the F9 function key. Then scan each ticket then cash out.

Utility Management

Item Classes

Found in Utilities Top Menu is the Class Manager. To add Categories for Items, enter this window and add the Code (single letter) and the Class description for each of the classes of items that you will add later. Make sure to add classes before Items.

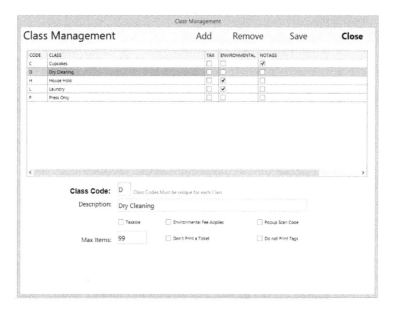

Item Manager

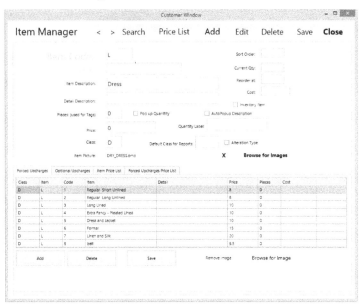

To get to item management select **Utilities** from the top menu then select **Item Management** from the drop menu.

Once an item is selected any related up charges will appear. If the Yes No Box check is selected in the Item Management screen for this Item, whatever is placed in the Description box of the up charge will appear in a Yes No Box forcing the use to select Yes or No on the Up charge

MULTI-LEVEL PRICING

Simple select the item you wish to create pricing levels for. Press the Pricing Level Button on the right of the window. A window will appear. Press add enter the level numbers and the prices for that item for that level.

I.e. Shirt (Laundry) is set as 1.25. Level 1 is set to 1.00 dollar, level 2 is set to .75 cents.
Then select each customer you wish to receive this new level and enter the pricing level for that customer in the F11 Customer Window. If an item that is selected for a ticket for that customer does not have a pricing level the system will default to the standard cost on the main Item Window.

Forced Up Charges

Forced Up Charges are similar to sub items. Use Forced up Charges to break items into detail groups. If you have an Item called "Dress" and you wish the counter person select a type of Dress then create the Item "Dress" then create Forced Up Charges for the types of Dresses. For example you can create a Forced Item called: "Formal Dress" and another called "Short Dress" and another Called "2PC Dress" each of these can have a different price and a different Piece count.

Optional Up Charge Manager

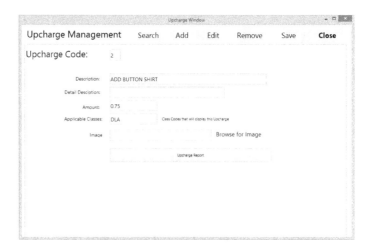

OPTIONAL UPCHARGE MANAGEMENT

You can manage this window from the Utilities – Optional Upcharge Menu

Note: When you select an Upcharge or a color the Enter Quantity of Items with this Upcharge will appear on the top with a spinner. The default quantity is equal to the number of items you entered. You may change this or select another upcharge or color. The quantity of items will appear on the ticket in (2) after the upcharge or color. If any additional cost are associated with the upcharge they will be multiplied by the quantity in this Enter Quantity of Items with this upcharge box.

Up charges must be assigned a unique letter, number or symbol on the keyboard and linked to a Class (Classes are groups of items. I.e. Dry cleaning,

Laundry or groups of items associated to a specific price list such as Dry cleaning for the Hilton Hotels) To assign an Up charge to a Class simple enter the class code in the Class field ie. If the existing item is assigned to class "D" for Dry cleaning and you would like the up charge to appear whenever a Laundry item is selected than append the "L" code to the list of class codes. The Class should look like this: "DL". Again if you wish to include the "H" class of items to the list change the class value to "DLH" (order does not matter – Uppercase does.).

User Manager

C To add users or change user access controls select the User Manager option from the top menu.

To **Manage** users select the user from the list then press the edit User button on the left.

To **Add** a new user press the Add User button on the left.

To **Remove** a user press the Delete Item button on the left.

- After you Add or Edit a user make sure to press the Save Changes button on the left.

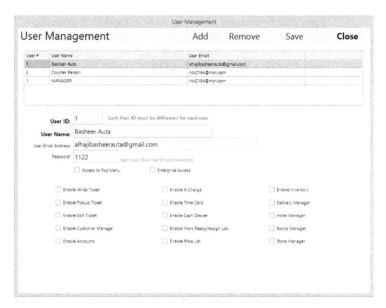

Each user requires a unique ID #. This number will be displayed on Tickets and transaction history. The User also requires a unique Password. Each user will enter the password # before transactions and when entering the program.

To allow this user to use the top menu for accessing reports and utilities place a check in the Access to Top Menu Option.

Enterprise access is used if you have several stores connected to your account and you wish the dashboard to access all you're stores.

Along with each user you must select which options you wish the users to have. Simple check the various options that apply to this user then press Save Changes. Each user can also have an email address separate from the store email address. This would be for email the employee.

Access Levels and Security codes are for reference only and not used in Follow Metro. This is a reference for compatibility with Legacy Follow Classic.

Report Customizing

Follow now has a 64 bit/ 32 bit Report Writer that is free open source and included in the Follow purchase. Go to Utilites and Select Report Writer and you will be able to customize all the reports in the Follow system. For assistance make appointments with Follow support.

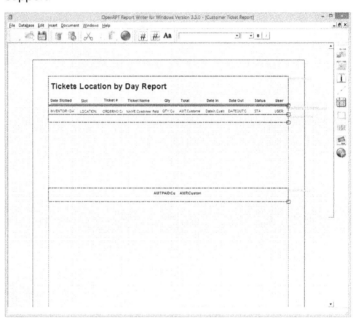

Ticket Properties

Customer Defaults

Follow will allow you to set default values for the basic customer information, such as City, State, Zip, default, and the default General Ledger Account. To enter these defaults you will need again to click the **Help** tab and enter the **System Properties** menu. Once in the system properties you will need to go to the **Advanced** tab.

Set Customer Taxable Default

To use the Tax Module you will need to modify two areas of the Follow system.

Step 1: From the top **Office** menu select the **Store Management**.

To set each new customer to default to Taxable you will need to check the "Auto set Customers to Taxable" in the Store Manager.

Then set the Tax Rate to the rate you wish to use as Tax. If a customer is non taxable then set the customer Tax option to unchecked when adding or editing the customer in the customer manager.

Access Control

To use **Access Control** you will need to turn on the following options:
Security and Access Control in Follow is comprised of three major modules.

The ability to create users and assign different levels of access. This is done under **Utilities** under the **User Management** menu.

Follow Metro requires a user to login when the application is open. Each user is assigned to a store as the user logs in and the menus will enable and disable with the users specified access. To modify the modules you wish the user to have access to open the User Manager under the Utilities top menu.

Then select the customer from the list and press the Edit User button on the left.

When the user menu appears select the modules on the bottom that you wish the user to have.
The buttons and the top menus associated with the item will appear and disappear when the user logs in.

Then if you wish the users to be forced to login again after a transaction is complete then return to the Store manager and turn on the "Use Login for each Transaction" checkbox

License Manager

Follow Metro does not require a license for each
client. Your monthly subscription allows you to use as
many clients free as you like. Just download the
client and upgrade from the FollowPOS.com site
install them on any computer. Your email address is
your license and will automatically login to the store
as you enter from any system around the world.

Archive Manager

Archiving is no longer needed with Follow Metro SQL
Server.

Clear Out Data

Clear out data is now done by the Follow Support
office. Please call for this to be done

X-Charge Application – Credit Card Processing

Follow Metro has built in credit card processing using
the x-charge processor. X-charge is a free PCI
compliant vendor who will process your credit card
over the internet. They supply their application free to
Follow users on a Month to month contract with no
termination fee.

To get a quote and signup call the x-charge office
today. Their number is located under contacts on our
website or in this manual. Let them know you are

signing up for Follow to get the Follow special rate and free software.

Once the x-charge software is installed, enter the store manager and turn on the option to Use Credit Card Processing and enter the path to the LocalTran folder in the Credit Card Path LocalTran.

Item Tag Management

The Garment can be managed in 3 different ways:

1. You can use preprinted Garment tags and enter the number on the final Print window. Follow Metro supports up to 8 tag per ticket. These are ranges so the first tag can be entered as GRN\01:01-03

2. You can print tags using the Epson u220 or the star sp 700 printers. These printers can be used to print tags at the same time that the ticket is printed. The tag will print the Ticket #, customer name and due date.

3. You can use thermal tags with barcodes to press onto the garment and use this to tag to scan each time the garment is brought in. (This requires you to purchase a thermal press and preprinted tags)

Email Notifications

To Setup the email system you will need to enter the email SMTP information under the Email Settings tab under the Store Manager. You will need to attain the

SMTP settings from your email provider. Remember that the emails send from the application will be actually send from your email provider allowing the customers to reply to your email directly.

For assistance call the Follow support office 760.282.4421

Follow Metro includes many features for emailing customers. To access the email modules select the Office menu then select the various email modules.

Email Reminders to Pick up Clothes

The most common email Follow sends is the overdue pickup clothes email. Select this module from the Office top menu. Set the date for the cutoff date, meaning that any tickets older than this date will send an email.

1. Set the date

2. Press the Show Tickets to display all the ticket that will trigger an email. (Emails will only be sent if the customer connected to the ticket has an email on file)

3. Press the "Send Email Reminder" button.

This screen will also send a personalized email to customer that have not been in the store for over 30 days. You can also modify the email body in the memo window on the bottom right. Then Press the "Send Missing Customer Email Over 30 days"

There is also a link to a website that offers suggestions on how to email missing customers.

Reclaim Old Customer Emails (example)

1. Send a "Re-introduction" campaign. The tone of the email is the most important factor here. Think more "Letter from the president" than "Boy, have we got an offer for you!!!!"
2. In that email, try to remind them how you got their contact information. If they've purchased something from your site, or if they've opted in, put that in your message. Got an order ID? Name of the product they bought? Mail-merge it in.
3. Give an incentive to stay opted-in. If I did business with you years ago, why would i want to do business with you again?
4. Send the re-introduction campaign to very small chunks of your list. Don't just blast one message to 9,000 people. Break it into smaller lists of 1,000 or 2,000. And why not spread it out over several days? That way, you can watch for abuse complaints, and tweak content for maximum effectiveness.

Follow also offers emails to new Customers. This option is under the Office – Marketing emails – New Customer Email option.

This window will send a custom email to customers who have just started coming to your store and will make the customers that the email has been sent so only one email is sent.

This window will allow you to modify the email then send. You can also enter your email and send a test email to you to view what it will look like. The email can contain html, but I recommend testing it before sending in that Html emails can be complicated.

This will also allow you export new customers to a flat file and export all customer emails to a csv file for exporting into constantcontact.com or mailchimp.com

Reports

Ticket Reports

Customer Reports

Marketing Reports

Multiple Store Management

Central Database Option

Cloud based - Your store data would be located on a Server located in the Cloud at a Hosting company. They make the database available to you anywhere in the world. They backup your data, manage your server and make sure it's available to you 24/7. You then can access your store anywhere in the world providing you have internet access. It's like being at the store from home, on the road, or anywhere. Change prices, run reports, look up tickets, see live production data and Reports, etc... All for $9.95 a month. Never worry about the computer dying and losing your data.

This option is great for absentee owners and multi-location companies. If you have a plant and dry stores consider this option to keep your Enterprise connected. To see if your internet is fast enough for the Cloud test the bandwidth (there are free bandwidth test sites that you can find on google.com. Make sure you have at least 5 download and 2 upload.

Multiple Store Inventory Tracking

Plant and Agency Setup

Cloud version is great for multi location setups. Talk with Follow Sales for a breakdown of how this works.

Database & System Backup

The hosting center for your data is winhost.com (follow them on twitter for system information and down information) They backup your data every night.

** If you choose the local database version of follow you will need to back up the data each night by your self.

Free Follow Internet Nightly Backups

The hosting center for your data is winhost.com (follow them on twitter for system information and down information) They backup your data every night.

Remote Access

Follow is Cloud based so you can access your data from anywhere in the World where there is Internet. Just download the Follow Client from www.followpos.com and login using your Email and password.

Training Videos

Training Videos are available at the Follow Training Web Site:

http://www.FollowPOS.com/videos.html

FAQ

- ## *Common Questions*

   o **What Kind of Hardware can be used?** Follow Metro can use Windows XP, Windows 7 or Windows 8 and can support 32 or 64 bit. Any computer that support these operating systems will work. We recommend at least 2 gig or Ram and at least 50 gig of Hard drive space available.

   o **What is price I have to pay to use Follow?** You have 2 plans to choose from. 1. Pay the Installation/Training up front with a setup charge of $395.00 per store and $9.95 a month. 2. Pay just $19.95 a month per store. This includes unlimited computers accessing that store for no additional charge. You can have 2 , 3 , 4, etc stations at your store for just one monthly fee and have a computer at home or laptop that you take on the road. This also include any laptops or tablets you might want to take on the road for delivery.

o **How much training do we get?** Training and installation is all done remotely using a programing called www.teamviewer.com that allows our techs to control your computer anywhere in the world. You get 2 hours of remote and phone training with a tech for each store. Also you get free unlimited email questions as well as online training videos.

o **Are there other fees?** No! Just the monthly fee of $9.95 or $19.95 per store. This also includes 1 hours of phone support per month for free. Additional tech support is $12.95 per 30 min increment.

o **What kind of internet will work with the cloud?** We recommend the faster the better. At least 5 upload and 5 download is preferred. DSL or Fios. Also make sure to use wired internet if possible. Wireless is always slower.

o **What printers will work?** Follow Metro Support primarily the Star TSP100 Thermal Printer, make sure to get USB printers in that new computers only have those connections.

o **Can the software print tags for the clothes?** Yes, we support the Star SP700 Impact tag printer. It must be USB and will need to be filled with Computer 3" tag roll paper from www.cleanersupply.com

o **Where do we pay the monthly fee?** You will be send a paypal invoice to pay on line each month. Or you can just go the packages link on the website and press the buy now button under the plan you have. ($9.95 or $19.95)

o **How do you get upgrades?** There is an upgrade link on the website. Jus click the upgrade link and Open then unzip. Make sure the program is closed on the computer you are upgrading. Each station must be upgraded separately.

Resources

Credit Card Processing through Follow X-CHARGE
Philip Head - 1202 High Tech Circle Henderson, Nevada 89015
www.Acceleratedpay.com
(800) 637-8268 x111
Fax:(702) 446-8145
philip.head@acceleratedpay.com

Hardware Quotes MS Cashdrawer
Tanya - 2085 East Foothill Blvd. Pasadena, CA 91107
www.mscashdrawer.com
Email Now Attn: Tanya Doubko
tdoubko@mscashdrawer.com
(800) 544-1749
Fax: (626) 792-4033
tdoubko@mscashdrawer.com

Follow Support Office
Email Now support@Followsystems.com
760-282-4421
support@Followsystems.com
Support Manager

Support Contract

Support Contract for Follow Systems

This Document is to purchase a support contract for the Cleaners listed below. Support is for 1 userUnlimited Stations at one location. License Serial Number _____. This support is transferable and can be resold. Support is for 1 year as of the date of purchase. All restrictions and warranties are referred to the Follow Warranty document.

Support entitles the user to:

1. Voice Support by a Follow Support Staff member. (Via Phone)
   a. Tech support will usually return calls with 24 hours. If it is an emergency you must state this in the voice mail or email correspondence. We will prioritize the call and place all emergencies first.
2. Free upgrades of the software
3. Link up service to your computer to view and fix issues via the internet. You must install the www.logmein.com client and have internet access for the computer(s).
4. Free user assistance via email or phone.
5. Phone support is limited to 10 hours a year for the base support price.
6. If there are hardware issues with the computer we will help you determine that and point you

to the hardware vendor for replacement or additional support. (i.e. Dell.com or Epson)

7. Follow Support only covers the use and functionality of the software providing that Windows, computer, and peripherals are running properly. The support contract is not a support contract for Windows or the computer or the Printers etc. You will be referred to the vendor for issues with those aspects.

    a. Software includes

        i. Follow Dry Cleaning System

        ii. The Report Writer (Includes training on writing reports and modifying existing reports)

        iii. The Database and the Database engine.

8. Onsite support for a daily fee of $150 a day (travel and expenses are billed to the customer separately) for one of the Follow Technical Trainers.

9. Enterprise Follow Support is for the Enterprise system and does include support for the SQL Database Server. (Remote Access is Required)

Price Paid: _____ Check No: _____ or Visa (Call)

Pricing - $199.00 a year for the first year of software use. $99 for each additional year

Per call support available on a per call basis for $12.95 per 30 min increment

Date of Support: _____

Support User's Name

_____

Cleaners Name

_____

Address

_____

City/State/Zip

_____

Phone for Contact:

_____

Follow Software Development Manager – Signature and Date of support

www.ingramcontent.com/pod-product-compliance
Lightning Source LLC
Chambersburg PA
CBHW071200050326
40689CB00011B/2190